MATT FEROZE

THE CHEESE AND I

An Englishman's Voyage
Through the Land
of *Fromage*

Complete and Unabridged

ULVERSCROFT
Leicester

First published in Great Britain in 2013 by
Michael O'Mara Books Limited
London

First Large Print Edition
published 2016
by arrangement with
Michael O'Mara Books Limited
London

A catalogue record for this book is available
from the British Library.

ISBN 978–1–4448–2904–4

SPECIAL MESSAGE TO READERS

THE ULVERSCROFT FOUNDATION
(registered UK charity number 264873)

was established in 1972 to provide funds for research, diagnosis and treatment of eye diseases. Examples of major projects funded by the Ulverscroft Foundation are:-

- The Children's Eye Unit at Moorfields Eye Hospital, London
- The Ulverscroft Children's Eye Unit at Great Ormond Street Hospital for Sick Children
- Funding research into eye diseases and treatment at the Department of Ophthalmology, University of Leicester
- The Ulverscroft Vision Research Group, Institute of Child Health
- Twin operating theatres at the Western Ophthalmic Hospital, London
- The Chair of Ophthalmology at the Royal Australian College of Ophthalmologists

You can help further the work of the Foundation by making a donation or leaving a legacy. Every contribution is gratefully received. If you would like to help support the Foundation or require further information, please contact:

THE ULVERSCROFT FOUNDATION
The Green, Bradgate Road, Anstey
Leicester LE7 7FU, England
Tel: (0116) 236 4325

website: www.foundation.ulverscroft.com

In 2011, Matt Feroze gave up his comfortable accountancy job for the chance to explore France and its wealth of cheeses. He learned the cheesemonger's trade from some of the best in the business, and carved a niche for himself in Lyon's famous indoor market as the Englishman who — contrary to common expectations — doesn't give terrible advice. In 2013, Matt won the title of *Champion de France* in the prestigious *Concours National des Fromagers*. He now lives in London with his partner Jen — and a fridge full of cheese.

Find him on Twitter — @MattFeroze

Contents

Contents

1

Bruno's Farm

Perched halfway up a mountain is La Ferme des Courmettes, a small collection of squat buildings, home to the enigmatic Bruno and his herd of goats. This was to be my home for the next few weeks.

The scraggy and fairly unforgiving mountain rises up just behind the coast of the Côte d'Azur. On a fine day you can see all the way along the voluptuous sweep of coast from Nice to the Cap d'Antibes, aware of the goings-on of that jet-set Mediterranean lifestyle, yet at the same time blissfully removed. So removed, in fact, that it's a gruelling one-and-a-half-hour trek through seldom-used forest trails to the nearest village.

In early March, the sky is generally that sort of heavy blue you rarely see in England, even at the height of summer, and the grass is green and vibrant as it covers the pastures in which the farm is nestled. The road leading up to the farm is dusty and potholed, with frequent sharp bends and sheer drops that cause beads of sweat to prickle out on the palms of my hands when they're taken at speed, which they usually are.

The area surrounding the farm forms part of a nature reserve, and Bruno's goats are allowed to graze freely — hairy little park keepers making sure the trees and the wiry undergrowth are kept in check with their insatiable appetites. Gnarled oaks and chestnuts spring up at all angles, and the undulating landscape is punctuated by rocky outcrops and clusters of small, bright flowers and wild thyme. It is hard to imagine an environment in which a goat could be happier.

Bruno Gabelier has made his home here since 1995. The isolated farmhouse is cramped, with only three rooms, and sparsely furnished. But it's warm; there's a comfortable, overstuffed sofa in the living room, and the kitchen is always full of fresh, local produce — food miles are counted on one hand here. It's not luxurious by any means, but at night the lights glowing from the windows across the dark pastures and hills can't fail to lift the spirits. Inside, Bruno likes to keep the television burbling away in the background. It often shows *N'oubliez pas les paroles*, the French version of the show *Don't Forget the Lyrics*. Bruno sings along, much to the disdain of the farm cat, who stalks through the house with a tubby aloofness.

Outside, along one wall, and extending out behind, is the long, low goat shed, its solid stone walls providing a foundation for the farmhouse in more than just a physical sense. Inside, on a straw-strewn floor, is housed a troop of eighty or so female goats, a few males and thirty precocious infants. These are Bruno's little earners. They are mostly of the Alpine Chamoisée breed: good milkers with a handsome brown coat, covered in black markings and flecks of white. They are well fed, healthy and full of energy. They are also inquisitive, playful and never, as I am about to find out, quite where you want them to be!

★   ★   ★

The 5 a.m. check-in at Gatwick Airport had taken its toll and the combination of sleep deprivation and a hastily snarfed Pret A Manger bacon-and-egg sandwich with large milky coffee was sitting uncomfortably with my stomach. I arrived into Nice airport at 9 a.m. in early March 2010, exhausted, bleary and disoriented. Nonetheless, I wasn't a complete stranger to this part of the world. I was feeling fairly confident that my experiences around Aix-en-Provence, where I had spent six months learning French a few years previously, would have prepared me well for navigating the rural bus routes to Grasse, the hilly home of French perfume. It was here that I was due to meet my new boss and landlord, Bruno. Bruno owned the farm on the nearby mountain and had, possibly against his better judgement, agreed to let me stay with him for the next four weeks, lending a hand around the farm and learning as much as I could about making cheese.

It was teeming with the sort of damp, generous rain that soaks you to the skin almost without effort. I sat in a bus shelter that smelled of mildew and old, fried food, listening to the rain drumming on the roof and hoping for a gap in the wet blanket of cloud above as I waited for the bus. It really was dismally cold. If it hadn't been for the Mediterranean, flat and grey as far as the inclement conditions let me see it, I could have been back in the UK.

Bienvenue à la Côte d'Azur . . .

Not for the first time I wondered if my friends had been right in raising their eyebrows or occasionally laughing outright at my choice of holiday. Employing my rusty French, I confirmed that the driver was heading in the right direction and took my seat as the bus started its slow meander through the countryside. I sent a text message to Bruno to let him know that I was on my way and started flicking through my old friend *French Grammar in Context*, perhaps vainly hoping to impress through faultless conjugation.

From Bruno's brief emails I had inferred a concern that I was some kind of soft-skinned, vacationing city dweller, clearly unsuited to existence in the wilds of southern France. I was ready to admit that to some extent his concern was valid: my first three years in the Big Smoke had not been kind to my waistline and, with the exception of a very small amount of indoor climbing, I really hadn't done anything approaching exercise for a long time. I was ridiculously keen to make a good impression, though, and confident that, despite recent lethargy, I had a solid background of wrangling with pigs and putting up with mud and ungrateful geese from my childhood on a rural Devonshire smallholding. I felt that I could prove that I wasn't all suits, cocktails and dim sum.

Suddenly, the realization struck that I hadn't put my watch forward on arriving in France and I got a sick, sinking feeling in the pit of my stomach. I had arrived into the airport at 9 a.m. English time, so 10 a.m. French time. I had told Bruno that I would be in Grasse at 11 a.m. That was ten minutes from now and he would be there waiting for me; I still had an hour's worth of journey left. So much for first impressions. *Merde*!

Following a grovelling text message, I arrived into Grasse bus station and waited for Bruno, who was nowhere to be seen. Every minute that I waited was heavy with embarrassment.

The car journey was awkward: Bruno's forgiveness was not immediately forthcoming and my level of comprehension was low. Bruno was gruff and serious, clearly a man of the countryside, a man of few, but carefully chosen, words. Strong forearms and a strong handshake complemented the pronounced odour of goat that emanated from him like an animal aftershave.

As he drove me up to the farm, he told me of its history, of the region and of his goats. Thankfully, I already had an understanding of most of what he was saying. Office work had finely honed my Google skills and, unlike many small farmers in rural France, Bruno had clearly made an effort to create an online presence, so my ear got a chance to adjust to his gruff, rounded French without getting too lost. He was a savvy man and had worked hard to craft the romantic image of the goatherd poet. He'd published at least two volumes of poetry, one of which contained some rather interesting sketches of nude women. He used these poetic offerings and the *berger*-poet title to promote his cheese in what was, I will happily concede, a fairly non-cynical way.

Bruno's farm was *bio* (the French version of organic), a choice that corresponded well to his philosophy of farming. But perhaps philosophy was too strong. He had a clear idea of how a goat should be raised and a cheese should be made, and it just so happens that this modus operandi fitted very comfortably with the requirements for the *bio* label.

In fact, it was precisely for the fact that the farm was organic that I was here, having acquired the contact details through a brilliant organization called WWOOF (World Wide Opportunities on Organic Farms), which was set up to help interested people learn about organic production methods by volunteering on farms in exchange for food and board.

Whenever he could, Bruno relied on the services of two WWOOFers to allow him to manage the farm, make the cheese, and go out and sell direct to clients and restaurants in the nearby towns and villages.

As we pulled up in front of the house,

Bruno informed me that the other WWOOFer staying at the farm was named Julien, and that he'd be around somewhere to help me get settled in. I shouldered my rucksack as Bruno drove off through the rain on what must have been important farmer-poet business.

Julien, a Canadian death-metal drummer with dreams of one day setting up an eco-village, was sitting in the living room, tapping furiously at the keyboard of an ancient desktop computer that looked as though it might have been powered by steam. (When it later stopped working, we took it apart only to find it full of goat hair and other assorted fluff. A quick vacuum-clean was surprisingly effective at getting it running again.) His thin, gangly frame was crowned by enormous quantities of unruly dark hair and a small pair of wire-rimmed glasses were perched on the end of his nose. These lent him a slightly bookish look that screamed librarian rather than rock star/farming enthusiast. He spoke quickly, and the French Canadian accent was new to me — new and rather incomprehensible. Thankfully, he seemed prepared to go easy on me, and after a while he broke into a heavily accented English to give my travel-furred brain a bit of a break. I sincerely hoped my ear would get reaccustomed to the French language quickly; otherwise this was going to be a bit of a slog for all concerned!

The presence of Julien on the farm was an immediate comfort. His passion for cheese, particularly raw (unpasteurized) milk, animal husbandry and organic farming was barely contained. Although his ideals were perhaps a bit more extreme than mine, we were clearly on the same spectrum of 'cheese love' and my choice to come here on holiday began to make a little more sense.

A fire was merrily blazing away in the corner, keeping the room snug with a pleasant smoky smell, and the fridge in the kitchen next door contained a truly inspiring amount of cheese. The rain lashing against the windows accentuated the cosiness of the little farmhouse, and I felt as if this was going to be a great place to spend the next few weeks — rustic and simple, certainly, but homely, too. I asked Julien where I was going to be staying, expecting him to show me upstairs to my room. Instead, he gave me a slightly wolfish grin and opened the front door, beckoning for me to follow him as he headed off down the track behind the house.

In the dark beneath the trees, propped up

on piles of bricks and creaking alarmingly in the wind, was a rusty and fairly unloved-looking trailer. It dripped uninvitingly in the rain as Julien bounded up to the door and flung it back on its hinges. Home sweet home. After pointing out the various creature comforts of my lodgings (bed, desk, cupboard on the brink of falling to pieces, minuscule electric heater attached disconcertingly to a mains connection), he retreated back to his room in the warmth of the farmhouse, telling me to come over once I'd got settled.

The trailer was freezing and damp, and the rain thundered on the roof. However, it was positioned close to the goat shed and even over the rain I could hear them. They bickered grumpily, stuck inside since play had been cancelled due to inclement weather, but even in their ill humour I found their snufflings, bleatings and the muted clanking of the bells they wore to be oddly soothing. They were the reason that I was here, and it was a pleasure to be living in such close proximity.

After unpacking my bag, which contained a few changes of clothes, a French grammar book and a recently acquired ukulele, I wandered back over to the house, where Bruno was still nowhere to be seen. In his absence, I asked Julien to show me the goat shed.

Goats are not docile animals; they need to explore and communicate. They have distinct personalities and a social hierarchy that is under constant evolution. To walk into a goat shed, with its almost overwhelmingly close, humid and animal smell, is to walk into a playground with its cliques, quirks, bullies and underdogs.

In Bruno's goat shed, the few males were corralled into a small pen. They had an aggressive look to them and huge horns protruded from the front of their shaggy heads. They were evidently not beasts to be crossed. While they don't get much opportunity to fraternize with the female goats in the winter, the numbers are clearly in their favour during the summer months: the three large males have more than eighty females to tend to, and every year each is father to dozens of kids.

It was clearly the females who ran the show here. They were the stars and they all had names, which Julien rattled off to me with impressive speed. That first night it was difficult for me to recognize them by sight, but before long their individual quirks became clear to me, and I could very easily tell them apart. When I first entered the shed, my eye was drawn to a pen at the far end bathed in the red glow of a heating lamp. Inside were about thirty baby goats. They were truly beautiful animals, heart-meltingly cute and already showing the mannerisms of their parents, even at only a few weeks old. The babies were tight bundles of energy with bright inquisitive eyes. They jumped immediately at our presence, falling over themselves in the hope that we had brought food and letting out little mewling bleats that sounded almost kittenish. Even though we didn't have any snacks for them, they were content just to try nibbling our clothes, boots and fingers with their warm, sandpapery tongues.

★   ★   ★

Dinner that night was a fairly quiet affair. Julien and Bruno were tired from the day's milking and herding, and my brain was still not quite up to speed with French conversation. We ate fresh, tangy cheese with hunks of warm bread in a silence that was, for the most part, comfortable. As I prepared to head out to the trailer, Bruno told me to help myself to any books from the rickety shelves in the lounge. I grabbed a volume in English about goat husbandry and bade them goodnight.

'If you need to use the bathroom in the

night, just watch out for the dogs,' said Bruno, moving to the couch and settling in. 'They might look cute but they're not pets. Christophe from next door only keeps them to protect his sheep from the wolves.'

'Wolves?'

'Yes,' he said elongating the word in case I had failed to understand, '*woolllvvves*. We'll need you at eight tomorrow for the morning milking. Goodnight.'

Wolves. Terrific. I found myself regretting that last large glass of water I'd had with dinner, and swallowed hard, hoping to be able to last the night without encountering packs of giant feral dogs, or their lupine relatives.

The mattress in the trailer was about as thick as a biscuit, but the blankets were warm and numerous and I burrowed into them, managing to make a fairly comfortable nest. Flipping open the book about rearing goats, I couldn't help but grin. On the inside cover was a faded ticket from Tiverton Public Library — a town about ten miles from the village in which I grew up. The unexpected connection to home was a comfort, and, even though my ears were straining for the prowling of wolves around the trailer, I fell asleep feeling ready to tackle my first day's farming.

2

A French Affair

My journey to Bruno's farm was fuelled through a desire to spend time in France — to travel but ultimately through curiosity to see how other people lived, or more accurately, how French people lived.

The seeds for my love affair with France were sown early by my parents, who had lived in Paris in their twenties. Throughout my upbringing, 'French food' was discussed with reverence. The stories of a cheap but good restaurant on every corner were numerous (and, at my then young age, slightly tedious). The adage that 'the English eat to live, the French live to eat' was regularly trotted out, as were the stories of the original Entrecôte restaurant, where people would be content to queue for hours to get a taste of that special, secret steak sauce.

Before I was born, my mother spent a summer as a private chef for a wealthy art collector near Saint-Paul-de-Vence, a small picturesque town really not very far from Bruno in the south of France. Living in the maid's quarters with an expansively plump and Bambi-eyed housekeeper called Maria, she had free rein of the kitchen garden and her own private chauffeur. The produce was sun-drenched and astoundingly fresh, and her little yellow notebook of recipes from that summer now sits on our kitchen bookshelves at home like an ingot of gold. As a child I didn't necessarily appreciate the style of the cooking contained within, but I implicitly understood its value.

It must have been completely maddening for her that I was such a fussy eater when I was younger: the only acceptable vegetables were carrots and peas and any kind of sauce was absolutely out of the question. If I'd been a bit more open-minded, maybe I wouldn't have missed out on some excellent cooking when I was growing up. I will be eternally impressed by my mother's flexibility and imagination in preparing food for me — it can't have been easy!

My father tells a story of how, shortly after their return to the British shores in the late seventies, he saw a television programme extolling the virtues of the microwave oven for cooking a whole chicken and how the brown skin of an oven-roasted bird could be mimicked with a generous layer of Marmite. Given that they had had the run of Paris and its gastronomic scene, as well as experience of how the wealthy Mediterraneans broke their bread, their reverence becomes rather understandable.

Food has always been important to us as a family, particularly the *origins* of food. This was led in no small part by my mother, who shifted from a vegetarian to a meat-eating diet through raising her own animals to ensure that the meat she put on her plate had had a 'happy life'. For as long as I can remember, we have kept hens in the garden, and in Devon my mother created a smallholding, producing large quantities of fruit and veg. From time to time we raised livestock such as pigs and geese, and for a short while we even had ownership of a particularly unruly goat named Dorothy — the quintessential example of a goat that was never quite where you wanted her to be.

So when, after university, I was looking for a new skill to add to my CV before entering the world of work, learning French in the south of France just felt like an immediately obvious and sensible thing to do. My parents had laid the groundwork for that decision long ago.

I visited a number of French towns, but Aix-en-Provence immediately appealed to me. It was a Provençal town not dissimilar in size to Durham, where I had spent four years at university, and similarly with a rather large student population. One of the big differences between the two, however, was the blissfully warm temperature — street-café culture in the beautiful but chilly northern English town just wasn't quite the same.

I had enrolled in a 'French for foreigners' course, run out of one of the many faculty buildings by a collection of well-meaning but rather disorganized teachers. I have to say that I have never enjoyed learning as much as I did in that period. I eagerly took every class, contributed excessively to group conversations, often did triple the required homework and generally set a new standard for obnoxious swottery. While I certainly didn't make the leap from flustered foreigner to elegantly fluent pseudo-French guy, by the end of the first month or so I was definitely able to navigate conversations without tying my tongue and my brain into too many knots.

I was staying with a friendly middle-aged French lady called Dominique in a knick-knack-riddled flat on the outskirts of the town. The room was comfortable (and, importantly, good value) and the location was ideal at just a few minutes' walk from the university. I was able to come and go as I pleased without feeling that I was getting in the way. Dominique was petite, with chin-length grey hair and a permanently made-up face, a tendency towards politically incorrect commentary and a slightly frustrating (although rather common) habit of linking the ability of others to speak her first language with their intelligence. The latter was unfortunate, given that she was a regular host to international students coming to France to learn or improve their French.

It must be said that she meant well and I am hugely grateful that she opened her home to me — the alternative would have been the significantly less enriching, and substantially more expensive, prospect of living alone in a studio flat. She also helped me massively with my French, refusing to speak a word of English despite, I remain convinced, being able to. When I arrived, I could barely get out yeses and nos, let alone complete sentences.

A massive plus to the living arrangement was the presence of Eric, an American student a few years younger than I, whose college had links to a school in Aix. He was learning the sommelier trade as an extracurricular activity and we got on well. Neither of our courses was particularly gruelling and we had plenty of time to enjoy the abundant student nightlife.

We found a bar in town that suited us well.

It was small, sparsely decorated and almost without exception completely empty apart from its three regular French customers and the barman, Aurelian. In a town with a lot of competition for student money, this bar was struggling pretty badly. We adopted it, becoming regular customers and making friends with the other locals.

A lot of my time and money went in that place but that was fine — I had a great time living like a student again. What was brilliant about being in France to learn the language was that, whatever you were actually doing, as long as you were doing it in French, it all counted as revision. I could always justify that drinking too much and chatting rubbish was like homework — it was improving my fluency, helping me tune my ear in loud, distracting environments and giving me the opportunity to practise the kind of French that they didn't teach at the school.

Midweek drinking was common, and I spent many an evening trying to impress French and American ladies, with varying degrees of success. Dominique certainly wasn't impressed when I rolled in at 8 a.m. as she was making breakfast one morning. But it was fine, I assured her: I had been out revising.

Eric also introduced me to the art of

buying wine, searching out the right bottle from the right *caviste*, or wine merchant, building up a good relationship with the retailer to ensure that you got good treatment — rather than simply picking a random bottle off the shelf.

There was, however, trouble in paradise — a significant sticking point that risked turning an otherwise perfect time sour. Dominique's cooking, which we were obliged to eat, was absolutely appalling. Seeing all the amazing fresh local fruit and veg, meat, cheese and wine all around us and not having access to it left me with a burning, unfulfilled desire to bury myself in this wealth of exciting food and food culture that I hadn't really appreciated before, despite my parents' best efforts.

The key factor in Dominique's choice of ingredients was price, and, to be fair, it would be hard to begrudge her for it. Everyone has to live within their means. But her repetitive repertoire of sad, limp vegetables and dubious meat was, well, distressing. One of the saddest moments of my time in Aix was when Eric and I discovered the shop where Dominique did her shopping — a grim affair humming with sterile strip lighting, where low-grade, industrially produced, pre-prepared monstrosities were stacked from floor to ceiling. These included the all-too-familiar (and frankly uneatable) frankfurter in puff pastry with excessive quantities of overly sweet béchamel sauce, of which Dominique seemed so inexplicably fond.

For balance, however, I should point out that I was not able to cook at that point, either. My university days had taught me little more than how to fry meat and then add a supermarket-brand cook-in-sauce (mm . . . creamy peppercorn), and at home my parents were very happy in the kitchen, so I didn't feel any desire to inflict my lack of ability on the rest of my family.

It is with an internal shudder that I remember cooking for Linda, my girlfriend at the time, when Dominique was away visiting family. Eric had made himself scarce and we had the flat to ourselves — the perfect occasion to woo.

Linda was stereotypically Swedish, with blue eyes and long blonde hair. She was energetic, opinionated and outgoing. We had met at the language school; she was in a class above me, having started a semester before I had. Although her English was fluent, and most likely better than her French, she never said more than a few words to me in English, and we stuck rigidly to communicating in French. This helped both of us a lot in terms of fluency, but had the unfortunate consequence that we were essentially developing a new language between us, which although it was *based* on French, I was not certain that a French person would have understood.

She was also vegetarian.

The vegetarianism put me completely out of my comfort zone; all those years of frying meat were useless to me and I had no other repertoire. In the end I served celery-and-blue-cheese soup (soup bought from a supermarket, cheese from the market and crumbled in when reheating) with a swirl of cream and a coriander leaf placed with a flourish in the middle, followed by pasta (supermarket spaghetti) with a pesto bought from the market stirred through it.

Hopeless, but at least it inspired me to learn to cook and never to embarrass myself like that again.

In all I spent six, fairly hedonistic months in Aix-en-Provence, doing a lot of the things that, as a disorganized chemistry student with a lot of lectures to attend, I had rarely found the time for in Durham. Along the way, I managed to pick up a good grasp of the French language and made a lasting friend in my trusty textbook, *French Grammar in Context*. We would sit up of an evening on the balcony, with a bottle of wine, a baguette and a Camembert, discussing the finer points of the *plus-que-parfait* (or the past-perfect tense), among other grammatical delights and gazing out over the adjacent car park in the warm Provençal sun.

★　★　★

I returned to the UK with a desire to learn to cook and to try to hunt out the best local food that Devon had to offer. Devon was the countryside, right? Vibrant and green with animals all over the place. There *must* have been some great local food.

My parents were supportive of my newfound desire to cook and my family leaned, more or less, on the generous side when critiquing my early efforts, which I imagine were pretty horrific. I became responsible for the family roast on Sundays (with a degree of executive control and consultancy provided by my father), read the majority of our family cookbook collection and started watching cooking shows on TV.

I was, however, frustrated. Exeter, at that point renowned for its almost complete lack of independent shops, seemed hopeless for picking up interesting wines and cheeses, *saucisson* (or sausage) and fresh vegetables, locally produced meat and fruit. The Crediton farmers' market was then a drab, sad affair. It provided little inspiration other than a great producer of tasty beef, who subsequently decamped to the upmarket Borough Market at London Bridge.

I've since learned that there is now a good, new independent cheese shop on the Crediton high street; sadly, though, it wasn't there when I needed it!

As a family, we had long ago given up on going to restaurants. With a few expensive exceptions, the establishments local to us were ghastly and thoroughly depressing — the kind of place that thrives only because there is no competition in easily walkable distance.

I had been spoiled by the colourful French markets, where quality was easily procured, and was supported by the local community. I had been spoiled by the presence of bakeries, pastry shops, wine merchants, cheese shops and butcher's shops (or, to give them their French equivalents, *boulangeries, pâtisseries, cavistes, fromageries* and *boucheries*) on every high street, and restaurants that provided quality and value.

Crediton's Tesco Express just didn't quite cut it, and soon enough it was time to move on.

★　★　★

I had heard things about WWOOF and WWOOFing from a friend — a talented musician with hippy-ish tendencies. He had spent a few weeks in France one summer ostensibly planting and picking vegetables and learning organic techniques, although, from the sounds of it, he spent more time smoking and enjoying use of the swimming pool. It sounded perfect. Given that I had only a limited amount of time available before the onset of what promised to be a sensible, grown-up career, I wanted to be able to get involved in French life immediately, to be able to practise my French and learn some new skills.

Browsing the WWOOF-France listings, I came across a number of interesting possibilities, including some goat farming in the Poitou-Charentes region of France, about halfway down the west coast. The required hours were long and the list of duties sounded gruelling and started very early in the morning. I'm now completely sure that this would have been a brilliant experience, throwing me head first and fully clothed into the deep end — full-on French immersion and new skills *à gogo*.

However, at that time, I'm ashamed to

25

admit, my desire for comfort won out. I instead chose an olive farm, billed as being mid-harvest, warmly located on the Côte d'Azur, where English was the spoken language and significant emphasis was apparently placed on sharing wine, conversation and good-quality food.

I arrived into Nice airport around midday in early October 2006, full of beans (mainly coffee beans), and excited about getting started and meeting my new hosts. The sun shone generously in the deep blue sky; the warm wind rustled the palm trees; and the drab Devon weather slid immediately into the far distance.

I was met at the airport by Robert and Lesley, who were both bronzed and impeccably coiffed and dressed. The welcome was warm as we made our way to their car, a big four-by-four with Monaco plates.

The olive farm was situated just outside Valbonne, a pretty, sleepy little town not far inland from Cannes and Antibes. It was a popular destination for UK second-homers, or those who had taken the plunge and emigrated. There were plenty of resources for the French-language-impaired, such as a bookshop and pub, although I did my best to avoid these, developing, as I was, a healthy thread of pretension in such matters.

The electronic gates opened on a lavender-lined road up to the house, the lavender's scent strong, its pale purple flowers in full bloom. To either side, on wide, grassily dishevelled terraces, olive trees rose at all angles, many gnarled and wizened with age and decades of selective pruning. The rich, dark green of their leaves contrasted against the blue sky and the deep character of their grey, knotted trunks.

We parked in the large garage, which hosted several cars, some of which were distinctly sporty. Rosemary bushes were everywhere and the borders of the large gravel-covered yard were vivid with colourful plant life.

My room was in an old grain tower, a squat, two-storey building nestled among the olive trees, with a circular footprint and a diameter of about 5 metres; it was comfortable and suitably appointed, and contained an *en suite* bathroom, which was ideal, as it was a little way from the house.

The house itself was small but perfectly formed. It was a retreat from Robert's and Lesley's busy city lives in the UK and the States and was therefore devoted to relaxation, hosting friends and food. There was no television, so, when attention was not directed towards either posing or solving the eternal dilemma of what wonderful thing we were going to eat that night, we talked, we read or we played Scrabble — we played a lot of Scrabble and for a short while I could remember all of the allowable two-letter words.

Food was taken seriously here and I was involved from the outset in preparing meals. Emphasis was on fresh ingredients, simply cooked. Lamb with garlic and rosemary picked from beside the front door was a staple, as were slices of squid marinated in ginger and chilli. Both were cooked quickly and effectively on the grill outside. There was always enough cheese.

The collection of cookbooks was slimmer than that of my parents but I devoured them with no less enthusiasm. My work requirements were far from onerous and I found that I often had whole afternoons to experiment in the well-equipped kitchen. I made my first eggs Benedict, complete with hollandaise sauce based on the *gastrique* method (usually a reduction of shallot and wine vinegar to provide a richly complex acidity to a sauce) rather than the far simpler addition of lemon at the end. I prepared a cottage pie, drawing on my father's inspiration of adding a rich cheese sauce over the cooled ragout-style meat before the mash is added and the dish cooked. I also recreated a dish that had served me well on many an inebriated evening back in Aix-en-Provence — the sandwich *américain*.

The sandwich *américain* is awesome in its simplicity. This is the Francification of the hamburger and chips, which is a stalwart of French kebab shops. The ingredients are largely unchanged, with the exception of the burger bap, which is replaced by half a baguette. This obviously changes the bread-to-burger ratio significantly and, if left like this, would represent something of a mean sandwich. The genius lies in adding the chips into the baguette, piling them high and swamping them greasily in the sauce of choice. To my mind this should clearly be French mustard and mayonnaise — I'll have no argument on this but will concede that, on occasion, harissa is an acceptable alternative to the mustard. It's a question of context.

My gourmet version of the sandwich with thrice the cooked chips, top-quality burger and homemade mayonnaise was epic. Actually, Robert and Lesley were away when I did this, and it's probably for the best. Despite my conviction of its excellence, I think it would have remained something of a hard sell.

★   ★   ★

My time in Valbonne was short, but it confirmed something hugely important for me: essentially that my desire to immerse myself in French food in Aix-en-Provence wasn't just a case of the grass being greener. The French really did seem to have access to food and drink of a quality that we didn't have in the UK, and certainly not in the part of Devon that I had grown up in.

Yes, it was expensive, but not exorbitantly so, and, if you didn't happen to have the flush of wealth associated with recent kidney removal and resale, you could still have a damn good time without the prime cuts and *grands crus*.

That said, the shopping bags that my wealthy hosts brought back from the market at Cannes were a sight to behold. Beautiful glistening fish, perfectly formed ceps (to be sliced and drenched in duck fat before grilling) and always a selection of high-quality raw-milk cheeses, to be appreciated over lunch with fresh salad, cured meats and fine southern wines served on a large wooden table out in the shade of the olive trees.

My love affair with French food had been born long ago, but in Valbonne it gained substance and understanding of what was possible. It grew from a childhood crush into a much more complex and satisfying relationship, one that would be with me for ever.

3

Weighing Up the Options

OK, so he likes France and he likes cheese. What on earth was he doing in the National Audit Office, then?

A sensible question, dear reader — I'll try to explain.

In the summer of 2004, I was coming to the end of my master's degree course at Durham. It was the culmination of four years' hard work (slog, on a bad day), through which I had learned a huge amount about my chosen subject. The most important thing that I had learned, however, was that my future career path was not going to be found wending its way through the world of chemistry.

I had worked hard and my grades were good, although not exceptional. My final-year project, which involved boiling cyanide-containing compounds in benzene, was well received and I was awarded the princely sum of £25 by BP for coming top ten in our year with my poster presentation — the first and last time that I earned money through chemistry. The final-year lab-based project had taken its toll on me, and I had come to accept that I just didn't want to know what happened when you boiled cyanide-containing compounds in benzene enough to justify the risk of actually performing the, frankly dangerous, experiment.

My university advisers were starting to talk about the possibility of further qualifications, but it was clear to me at this point that, despite the undoubted coolness of getting to be called Dr Feroze, it just wasn't enough return on the investment of three or four years of my life to study for a PhD.

It just so happened that, during this time of uncertainty about my future (which all would have agreed had previously looked pretty chemistry-flavoured), my father had been given the green light on a contract providing imitation-marble columns for a private residence in the hot, dusty Indian town of Pune. He needed someone with experience to go out there and oversee the work of a group of Indian marble workers, and I, having spent many a university holiday polishing columns in his Devon workshop, was potentially the man for the job. The money was good and the prospect of travel strongly appealed — as did the opportunity to put off making any serious career decisions for six months or so.

India did not disappoint. It was both beautiful and heart-wrenching, and the experiences taught me that I actually could rely on myself in difficult situations. It gave me a huge confidence boost.

The house we were building columns for belonged to one of the local Indian elite. This insight into how the other half lived provided a shocking perspective on the relative poverty of the majority of the town's three million or so inhabitants. The learning curve was steep, and the work hard and crazy, but we got the job done.

I do not for a minute deny that I was exceptionally privileged to have this opportunity. My daily expenses allowance was sufficiently generous for me to explore almost everything that the town had to offer, particularly in terms of the food. This was often hot, always heavily spiced, and the quality of those spices, coupled with the understanding of the Indian cooks, has spoiled every subsequent curry that I've tasted in England — with the possible exception of Tayyabs near Whitechapel. That's not to say that there weren't some downsides in India, curried turkey on Christmas Day being a perfect example, and I never could get the hang of spiced breakfast.

I have very fond memories of sitting,

hidden from the overpowering sun by the shade of the bizarre Medusa-like Banyan trees, and drinking large quantities of Kingfisher beer. Happy times!

After finishing the job, I travelled around India zigzagging from Mumbai down to Kerala and Tamil Nadu. Food was always on the radar, as was beer — the perfect way to cool down burning lips. I tried hot Goan fish curries while living in a beach hut suspended on stilts among palm trees, and soothing rich, creamy Keralan cooking on a two-day houseboat journey through the vibrant green coastal backwaters. Ironically, the dish that caused me the worst stomach upset was a bowl of banana porridge in Hampi, a spellbinding, wild, boulder-strewn expanse with an ancient temple at every turn. Sometimes you just crave a bowl of something unspiced.

Travelling in India was hard; the poverty everywhere was draining and highly distressing. I had real trouble knowing how to address it, how to go about enjoying my experiences in the face of a significantly lower value placed on human life. I was struggling with the way that I was reacting. Being a relatively wealthy tourist resulted in a lot of hassling from the locals and I found myself often haggling over tens of rupees, the equivalent of a few pence, and then hating myself for it.

After a couple of months, this feeling of uncomfortable guilt, coupled with the ever rising temperatures from the rolling on of spring into summer, pushed me out, and I flew to New Zealand. There, I enjoyed the freedom of an open-ended return ticket, a reasonably healthy bank account and the strong English pound. Backpackers were well catered for and there were plenty of interesting activities, such as the obligatory skydiving, which I am glad to have done but would not care to repeat.

A few months later and I was just about ready to return to the UK. Well, I say 'ready', but it would be more accurate to say that my bank account was no longer quite so healthy.

But I still didn't feel ready to jump into a career, mainly because I didn't know what I wanted to do; and, what's more, I had no understanding of how to go about deciding what I *did* want to do. So what to do next? Back to Crediton and polishing columns I went, calling once again on the hospitality of the long-suffering parents.

My first experiences of travelling had opened my mind to the possibilities of living in other countries, and it was this that really motivated me — the idea of spending time in a foreign land learning another way of life, rather than passing through and leaving with a pretty photo album. It was this desire to integrate that led me to Aix-en-Provence and subsequently Valbonne.

⋆   ⋆   ⋆

The auditor-shaped piece of the puzzle came into being in between my time in Aix and that spent on the olive farm in Valbonne. I had come to the startling realization that I was soon to be three years post-graduation with what was starting to look like a very empty CV. I realized that I needed to get into a graduate scheme quickly, as these allowed employment based on transferable skills of the land picked up in extracurricular university activities, rather than having actual bona fide experience in a given industry. I hadn't been the secretary of the Durham University aikido club for nothing after all.

My grades put me in a relatively strong position for job hunting, although at the time there weren't a huge number of positions out there. I spent much time soul searching, a fairly large proportion of my time playing computer games and the rest of it learning how to cook and hunting out nice things to eat. After a month of almost no progress, it was clearly time to change tack: I decided that, if I didn't know what I wanted to do but needed to do *something*, it might as well be something that I was good at.

I performed what in retrospect can only be termed a skills audit (how appropriate!) and narrowed down my options to consultancy and accounting. My fledgling love of food and food culture was something that I wanted to keep as a private interest to nurture, so, after some deliberation between the two career paths, the accountancy won out. I found that the organization of numbers and figures could be immensely satisfying, and there would be a substantial amount of extra learning associated with the position. While further study in the field of chemistry had left me cold, I missed studying in general and I was keen to get back to the books.

I had run into the 'big four' accountancy firms at careers fairs and, while they had slick sales pitches, I struggled to see myself fitting into their image. I was taken instead by the possibility of a public-sector role, and, with that in mind, I applied to the National Audit Office.

The NAO application was in fact one of my first, and started more as a trial to see if I could get some interview practice. I have vivid memories of the interview process, particularly the first question.

'Hello, Matt, my name's Sharon,' my interviewer said in a friendly, assuring manner before immediately slapping me with, 'So what do you consider to be the three main factors in change in the public sector at the moment?' Even after the best part of five years' employment with the NAO, I still don't think I could give a particularly coherent answer to that question. I muddled through, though, and made it to the second round of interviews a few weeks later. I was told to prepare a ten-minute presentation on faith schools and to be ready to answer questions on the subject.

I had arrived in London the evening before, hoping to be well rested in time for the interview at 9 a.m. the next day. Once I'd settled into the rather dingy Pimlico hotel and had had a quick run-through of my presentation with papers spread out across the desk, I went out in search of food.

Victoria Station was grey and busy and there was an end-of-days-style thunderstorm kicking off. I had a distinctly sub-average meal at a French chain restaurant in the station and headed back to the hotel, trying my best not to get drenched by the taxis and buses as they thundered through the puddles.

On opening my hotel room door, I found

water dripping through the ceiling in the corner near the window. I informed Reception, who said that they were full and offered me a discount and a towel to mop up the water. I'm not quite sure why I accepted the offer, but I did, and so I returned to my room, towel in hand. I was greeted by a rather impressive indoor water feature pouring from the ceiling onto the bed, the floor and, of course, my notes for the following day, which were by now utterly ruined.

I left at 10 p.m. in the pouring rain in search of a new hotel, dishevelled and clutching the sodden pulp that was my presentation.

Despite the harrowing experience of the night before, the interview day breezed by, and I even had fun, bonding with one of the directors, whose fascination with Italy and its food culture reflected mine for France.

When the job offer came, I didn't hesitate. I knew that I would get on well here and was very happy to accept the offer. That said, I did defer my start date so that I could go to Valbonne before succumbing to a grown-up career of spreadsheet juggling.

★ ★ ★

I started work in January 2007 and was immediately carried away with it. There was a huge amount of training and document signing, followed by tight revision schedules for the 'early hurdle' exams, so called because failing them resulted in the early termination of the training contract.

Work on clients was divided into bite-sized chunks and I was involved in a large number of different projects, involving a fair amount of travel, some national, some international. Some of the locations I got sent to were rather glamorous (Strasbourg), and some distinctly less so (Swindon).

The role of the NAO is to audit the accounts of the UK governmental bodies that spend taxpayers' money, and to perform a number of studies on value-for-money issues — resulting in its reputation as a 'government watchdog' in the press.

While there is a large amount of pretty serious work involved, the role of the auditor is essentially to confirm that the audited entity has prepared its accounts correctly. This is done by talking to people about the work that they do, checking thoroughly that they have done what they've said they have done, and creating complicated spreadsheets with many, many different colours.

I moved to London in early 2007, renting a room in the top half of a beautiful, converted, Victorian terraced house on a quiet leafy street in Tufnell Park. The location was perfect: it was not far from the Tube, it was calm, and my room looked out into the garden, which formed part of a large triangle made by three adjoining terraces. With several trees in the centre, when I looked out of my window, it was hard to believe that I was in a city at all. It was fantastically cheap, too, and, while I did definitely have the feeling that this all might be too good to be true, it didn't stop me from taking the room.

My landlady and housemate was Juliet, a middle-aged lady of good upbringing with an occasionally nervous disposition and seemingly limitless reserves of vocal enthusiasm, delivered in a way that seemed almost as though she were trying to convince herself more than others.

Juliet was an artist, and would frequently pronounce the word 'aaaaah-tist' for extra emphasis and reverence from her audience. Now, I must add here that I know very little about art, so my opinions are entirely uneducated and shouldn't be taken too seriously.

Juliet was very keen to welcome me into her home, and to share her 'space' with me. There was much of her work around, but she only imposed one canvas on me — it was a monster! One and a half metres tall by at least three metres wide and too big and heavy to affix to any of the walls without its becoming a major operation that neither of us was quite prepared to invest him- or herself in. We left it sideways, propped up against the wall, but it was substantially taller than the height of the room, so it jutted out at an angle and took up a huge amount of space. The canvas was largely empty, with the exception of some colours arranged into what was fairly obviously (abstractly speaking) a tree, and a black smudge in one corner that was, I later found out, a dog. I lived in fear of damaging this prized work, and depriving future generations of its beauty.

Juliet's kitchen was very well appointed and it was here that, drawing on the aid of the food writer Nigel Slater's oeuvre, I learned a lot about cooking — it was the first time that I was really fending for myself. The concept of the kitchen, she told me with evident pride, was 'city living', which apparently translates to attractive fittings, a very small fridge and almost no cupboard space. Ergonomic? Yes. Practical? No.

The relationship between us was sometimes difficult — Juliet never managed to persuade me that mouldy fruit was art, I never managed to persuade Juliet that she didn't need to keep every newspaper clipping or magazine that she had ever purchased — but on the whole we got on well. I stayed for eighteen months in the end, enjoying settling into London, going out and exploring — when not revising for exams, that is.

In the summer of 2008, I moved south of the river, where most of my friends lived and where there was also a significantly less traumatic commute into work. I soon realized how spoiled I'd been by Juliet's luxury townhouse, and, after viewing the fifth or sixth minuscule room in houses that had obviously seen better days, I eventually plumped for a house share in Battersea. It was an ex-council three-bedder, and I would be sharing with two girls — who quickly became differentiated in my mind as nice Louise and mean Nicola. Mean? Let's just say that on my first night in the house she was having a Wimbledon finals party, Pimm's, barbecued meat, etc. It was made very clear that I wasn't invited. That night I sat in my room eating Stilton on toast counting down the days until she moved out, which, thankfully, would be in a few weeks' time.

Nicola left a legacy of nicotine-stained furniture, intimidating letters from the numerous organizations to which she was in debt, and a very large pile of voter-registration forms for the local area that were inexplicably under her bed. Louise and I were now in the position of finding someone else to move in.

Over the course of three evenings, we had about twenty people turn up to view the room, often at the same time. The last two people were scheduled for 6 p.m. on a sunny July Wednesday. I answered the door to an out-of-breath girl with a cloud of reddish curly hair. 'I need to get to grips with London distances,' she said, panting slightly. 'I've just practically had to sprint all the way up Lavender Hill to get here on time. Do you mind if I have a glass of water before I fall down? I'm Jen, by the way.'

I smiled and invited her in. As I was getting her a glass of water, the doorbell rang again, and Louise opened it to find a waxy-skinned man wearing beige leather trousers and an enormous Mohican that I was pretty sure could be used as a dangerous weapon. Louise shot me a stricken look, before introducing me hurriedly to the guy at the door — whose name I hadn't quite caught but thought it sounded something like 'Auntie' — and ushering Jen through to the lounge. Guess I'd be doing the interview with the possible axe murderer then. Excellent. Auntie was, it turned out, Finnish. His grasp of English was patchy to say the least. After he'd drilled me on how to pronounce his name (that didn't go well, by the way), the flow rather dried up until he bizarrely broke into a soliloquy in the bathroom about how passionate he was about cycling, while staring at me without blinking. I promised to let him know our decision in a few days, and then gratefully closed the door on his way out, resisting the urge to bolt it behind him.

Jen moved in the following week. She was fresh out of Cambridge and about to start a job in children's publishing. She had big hair and a big laugh, an enthusiasm for all things French and a love of food — we got on immediately.

Shortly after Jen had settled in, Louise gave a set of keys to her boyfriend so that he had somewhere to stay while looking for his own place. She hadn't told us, and I'm going to be honest and say that it came as something of a surprise to have a well-built man significantly over 6 feet tall let himself into our house. He was friendly enough but it was immediately clear to Jen and me that he had no intention of leaving and had an annoying habit of taking control of the TV remote and watching endless football matches (might be worth mentioning at this point that I'm not hugely into sport), as well as raiding the fridge, not doing the washing-up and — most heinous of all — eating the last of the nice biscuits.

Jen and I bonded strongly over our shared annoyance at his continuing presence; we went to the pub, went out for meals and generally hung out away from the house when he was around. We were, essentially, dating, and one night after many mojitos and, somewhat inexplicably, a cut-throat game of bowling at the Trocadero in Piccadilly, we decided to make it official.

Later, we moved into a flat together near Clapham North — a two-bed, first-floor Victorian conversion with a tiny kitchen and a master bedroom that looked out over the busy train line cutting past the Battersea Power Station and into Victoria. Though sometimes noisy, it was our home and it was bright and comfortable. I was happy in London — feeling settled with a loving relationship, a reasonably well-paying job and a pretty active social life. I was able to explore the town and graze wherever and whenever I fancied. I acquired my own collection of cookery books, a credible wardrobe and what was starting to become quite an expensive cheese habit.

Work was hard and time-consuming, and revising for exams had rather eaten into my plans for holidays. My journey to the farm began, as all the best stories surely do, with a memo from the Human Resources Department. There had apparently been a large build-up of accrued leave across the office and it was clear that some of us weren't getting the rest and recuperation that we required. The word from on high was less crassly phrased than 'use it or lose it' but the underlying message was the same.

I immediately booked a month off and set about deciding what to do with it. It wasn't long before I was back on the French WWOOFing site again, and, after a few evenings of browsing, I found something that looked to be right up my street: a small goat farm near Antibes, run by a guy named Bruno.

4

A Day on the Farm

The daily needs of goats are fairly predictable. As farm life revolves around the needs of the goats, our daily routine is therefore also fairly predictable. For me this is no bad thing, particularly over this relatively short period. I find that there is a pleasant relief in not being professionally, and all too often emotionally, involved in long-term projects (i.e. audits stretching over several months). When the work is done for the day, it really is done. There are no extra tasks that can be performed to usefully advance the farm for the next day. The work may be physically demanding at times but this is a small price to pay for the immense satisfaction of being able to put your feet up without the nagging doubt as to whether or not you really are on track for your deadline.

By comparison, working all day in the office has a tendency to leave me feeling podgy, mentally tired and totally uninterested in doing anything useful with my evenings. My time on the farm was very productive: I read an enormous amount about cheese production, goat handling and French grammar, and I played a lot of ukulele. But I have to confess that, despite the attention given, the French grammar and the ukulele playing did not see significant improvement — I mastered REM's 'Losing My Religion' and about half of 'Wonderful Tonight', a rendition about which I'm not sure Mr Clapton would be wildly thrilled.

The early mornings at Bruno's were fine, probably due to the early nights and the almost complete lack of alcohol. I was even sleeping well tucked up nice and snug in my trailer, which, after we had become properly acquainted, suited me perfectly. It had fewer mice than my London bedroom (I had left Jen battling an invasion of particularly brazen rodents back in Clapham) and the added advantage of not backing onto a busy railway line.

We had a definite daily routine. I would wake up at around seven in the morning, shower and grab some breakfast before Françoise, Bruno's employee, arrived. We'd aim to have hot, strong, black coffee ready to go as her little car came into view on the winding mountain road. From my combined experiences of working in France, the country is essentially powered by regular doses of strong black coffee. When someone does something stupid, an oft-heard commentary is, '*Il n'a pas eu son café*', or, 'He clearly hadn't had his coffee'.

The first task for the day is to greet the goats. They are already awake and bleating their morning gossip. They come to meet us at the gate to the shed, eager for food and the chance to get out and forage. We enter, often climbing over a gate rather than opening it, reducing, but never truly eliminating, the possibility of escape attempts.

The shed is dark and heady with the smell of goat — humid, warm and richly animal. The floor is deep with a mixture of straw and picked-through hay that the goats have trampled and thus no longer consider to be edible — goats have high standards when it comes to hay.

We corral the goats into a kind of makeshift, pre-milking holding pen to ensure that they all get milked and also to give us the opportunity to fill the now empty mangers that line the long interior stone walls. I like to think of this pen as the backstage area. The girls know what's coming next and are eager to line up in front of the door to the milking room; the more boisterous among them push and shove for a coveted position in the first wave.

The milking room has an elevated, enclosed runway and the goats enter stage left; they are lined up — via a relatively complicated system of levers and bars — with one hungry head per feeding trough. The feeding troughs face away from the audience, who are instead treated to a view of udders, the like of which Spearmint Rhino has probably never seen.

Electric milking pumps are used and, once you get the hang of it, the goats are quickly exiting stage right with empty udders and a spring in their step. Depending on the current meteorological conditions they head either to the sunshine and green pastures (cue much frolicking and climbing on things), or back in the shed to the mangers (cue sullen skulking and much sorting through hay).

Well, sometimes that's how it works. Often however, there are problems. As I said before, goats are never quite where you want them to be.

Rather than the neat row of udders, you might be unlucky enough to find yourself with one goat straddling the others, or underneath, or two stuck in the same spot, or one facing the wrong way — with goats, the possibilities for snarl-ups are endless. The resulting mess is akin to goat twister, with heads and feet everywhere. Your helpful advice is thoroughly ignored, and your well-intentioned limb manoeuvring will be received entirely ungraciously.

Sometimes, when you think that the cast are all backstage, they aren't. A few of them might have tired of waiting and chosen to take a leap over the barriers in search of hay. Goats are awesome little jumpers.

Then there's the hand-milking. Mothers who have recently given birth produce colostrum, a form of milk rich in proteins and antibodies which, although great for the immune system of a newborn, plays havoc with the coagulation process in cheese making and must not be allowed to get mixed up in the rest of the milk. New mothers are given a stylish green collar so that we know to milk them by hand (the core of the milking troop have a zippy orange collar instead). The green-collared are milked into a bucket. This is a knack that you have to pick up fairly quickly, the hardest element being ensuring that the goat doesn't either put her foot in the bucket or, worse, kick the bucket over, covering you in sticky warm milk.

Oh, and I probably ought to mention the requirement to hunt for and remove any ticks that might have found their way onto the udders during the goats' mountainside strolls. All for the love of cheese!

Once the goats are empty, we send the morning's milk (combined with that taken the evening before, which has been left at a low temperature to allow bacteria to develop slowly overnight) to the cheese-making room just down the hill, where its subsequent treatment depends on the type of cheese that we're making.

Time now for a quick cheese-making interlude . . .

Milk is a liquid with sugars and minerals dissolved in it, and fats and proteins suspended in it. The fats and proteins are in the form of microscopic globules and spheres that are soluble only within a narrow range of acidities. If you take the milk outside this range, the proteins that make up the neat spheres unravel like balls of wool and get tangled together in a big lump. This is the curd. You can achieve this effect yourself by pouring lemon juice into a saucer of milk. The milk will split forming curds (the lumps) and whey (the liquid).

More commonly, however, the acidification comes about not through the addition of acid but by bacterial action. The bacteria natural to the milk, or those deliberately introduced to the milk from a carefully chosen culture, consume the lactose sugar in the milk, converting it to lactic acid. As the lactic acid

54

concentration increases, so does the acidity, until the milk splits. This you can also achieve at home by leaving milk in the fridge for too long. Eventually, you will have curds forming. The reason why this is horrible and cheese is nice is all down to the type of bacteria that are doing the work — let's just say that what's happening in your milk bottle is not the action of a carefully selected bacterial culture.

This process is known as lactic coagulation and it results in a fragile curd that gives an often slightly brittle, chalky texture in the finished cheese. Small goat's cheeses are usually great examples of this. These cheeses don't respond well to a long ageing period and are typically at their best when aged around three to seven weeks.

The other type of coagulation is less easy to carry out at home. It is essentially the enzyme-controlled breakdown of the proteins (caseins) and their reformation into a reasonably ordered network, or gel. The enzyme used is known as rennet, which is found in the stomachs of young mammals, allowing them to extract the nutritional elements of the milk to better digest them.

This is rennet coagulation. These cheeses tend to have a smoother nature to their texture, although that's not always to say they're creamy. If you think about the smooth, slightly flexible texture of Comté, Emmental or Cheddar, you're on the right track. These cheeses tend to be better suited to significantly longer ageing periods, anything from months to years.

Rennet coagulation is typically fast, maybe around an hour or so dependent on the concentration of rennet and the temperature of the milk. A lactic coagulation is slower: around twenty-four hours might be required for the bacteria to do their thing. A combination of the two can be performed to produce a mixed coagulation, using a lower concentration of rennet and resulting in a longer time for curd formation. Camembert is a good example of this category.

Ultimately, all cheeses fall somewhere on the scale of lactic/rennet coagulation; the cheese maker chooses where on that scale to control the properties of the final product.

Like many goat farmers, Bruno essentially makes two kinds of cheese. He makes a range of lactic cheeses to sell during spring and summer, when the high-quality fresh milk is readily available. Alongside these, he makes larger, rennet-based, pressed cheeses (often described as tomme) which he can keep to sell during the winter months once the goats have reached the end of their lactation cycle.

After finishing the milking, we head down

to *la fromagerie* and don protective cheese-making uniforms (boots and heavy aprons) to start on the cheese making. The requirements for the day will be noted for us on the whiteboard. The type of cheese that we make on a given day is varied according to orders and Bruno's estimation of market and restaurant demands. Generally, however, we make the lactic curd-based cheese for which he is best known. He makes a selection of different shapes: some are rolled in vegetable cinders, others are made with a powerful pesto or tapenade through the centre. All are sold fresh though — often only days old. The cheeses are goaty, but not overpowering in flavour, with herb and grass notes and a pleasing acidity that leaves you wanting more. The texture is fragile and gives way easily to the cheese knife.

My personal favourite among these (and I'm not the only one) is the fresh cheese with the strip of pesto through it. The combination of basil and soft, fresh goat's cheese borders on divine. All it needs is some texture, such as a warm, crusty baguette, to make this the perfect lunch.

Today we're making a batch of fresh, lactic cheeses. The milk has been fermenting overnight in plastic tubs. We test the surface to judge the quality of the set, looking for a uniform texture and a clear separation of the curd from the insides of the tub, showing off nicely the clear whey. We empty most of the whey into a waste pipe that sends it straight to a trough outside for the goats. This never fails to generate a bleating and clanging stampede because they can't get enough of the whey, and I don't blame them: it's sharply acidic but with a pleasing hint of sweetness to it.

The curds are then carefully ladled into small moulds called *faiselles* on a big sloping aluminium table. The moulds are full of holes designed to let the additional whey run off. We take scoops from the top and bottom of the curd, alternating with each layer. Gentle ladling respects the delicate curd and gives a finer texture in the finished cheese. The top of the curd is usually more firmly set than the bottom, which is wetter with whey. We try to ensure that both are split evenly between the moulds because, even with a farm cheese, we have to strive to create a relatively uniform product, as the client demands it.

Over the course of an hour or two, sufficient whey has left the moulds to reduce the size of the bright, white, nascent cheeses by half. At this point they are removed from the moulds and rotated before being returned to them. This is fiddly as the soft white cheese is crumbly and delicate and often refuses to turn over neatly. It's one of those actions that a trained hand performs with the ease and confidence that derives from substantial experience, making the action look simple yet elegant, like a butcher tying up a roasting joint, or a department-store worker wrapping a present.

Even after three weeks at Bruno's, I succeed in making this action look neither simple nor elegant, but I get the job done nonetheless.

With the cheese made and unmoulded, we clean up and head out.

In fine weather, the goats are let out to play, and the mountain is their playground. My favourite part of my time on the farm is when I am following them. I would like to say that we herd the goats, but in reality they have little need of us, and we tag along for the ride. I took immense pleasure in watching them forage and explore. We would start off along the winding mountain road and then at some point branch off onto the wooded slopes in search of tasty pickings. There was a lot of goat, and we couldn't really control it. It was the perfect occasion to sit back against a tree in the sun and butcher the *Tetris* theme tune on the ukulele. They came and went as they pleased, feasting on the abundant vegetation around us.

★ ★ ★

Bruno spends some of his time working in a cooperative shop set up by local producers to allow them to sell direct to the public and, at the same time, to share the burden of taking time out to work in a shop. This kind of outlet is crucial for producers of their ilk: not only does it allow them to keep the supply chain (and therefore margin sharing) to a mini-mum, but it also reduces the need for the usually untenably high fixed cost of an employee.

Bruno is a rarity in these parts for actually having an employee, Françoise, who generally takes care of the daily farm work, liberating Bruno to market and sell as much as possible. Between them, they even manage, on very rare occasions, to take some time off for holidays.

5

The Birth of a Cheese Evangelist

Jen hadn't been able to take a whole month of leave to join me and, let's face it, even if she'd had a sufficient holiday due to her, it was highly unlikely that she'd have chosen to spend it gallivanting with goats halfway up a mountain. However, I managed to negotiate a couple of days away from the farm, and she flew out to join me for a long weekend near the end of my stint with Bruno.

We had arranged to meet in Nice and travel to Antibes, then back to Nice before she flew home again. The weather was hot and sunny. You would have mistaken it for a UK summer if the sun hadn't attacked the eyes at that slightly blinding angle.

I was waiting for Jen at airport arrivals, with my two-and-a-half-week beard and delightfully ingrained goaty odour (and no, dear reader, it wasn't that I hadn't showered: the goat smell is brutally hard to shift). We had spoken relatively little on the phone over the last three weeks. The signal was never great and the crackly international calls were frustrated by regular dropouts. To make matters worse, my access to technology had been significantly limited owing to the goat fluff build-up (the vacuuming of the computer came relatively late into my stay), so even organizing where to meet and what sort of holiday we'd have had been slightly trickier than anticipated. Nonetheless, it all went off without a hitch (goat stench notwithstanding) and we spent a few glorious days exploring the two coastal cities.

If Antibes were a person, it would be a distinguished old gent with a twinkle in his eye. The old part of the town gleams with white stone buildings and stately arches, through which the harbour glints a deep blue. We wandered along the ramparts and then up a fairly gentle wooded hill slightly out of town to the old lighthouse, where we had an early lunch of Saint-Félicien cheese that was creamily oozing out of its waxed paper and crying out to be mopped up with some crusty bread. We'd also bought a bottle of wine, a rich but not overly sweet, deeply coloured rosé, so we sat in front of an old white church on the top of that hill, looking out over the beautiful Mediterranean and rather sheepishly swigging our rosé de Provence straight from the bottle. Who travels with wine glasses?

We had a great couple of days in Antibes. A particular highlight was an evening in an absinthe bar, where a smiling woman named Agathe instructed us on the correct and bizarrely complicated way to get acquainted with the 'green fairy,' as this drink is often called. She was small and plump, with dark-brown hair pinned back into an elaborate up-do that looked at least as solid as cement and would almost certainly have put her at serious risk around a naked flame. Patiently, she showed us how to work the traditional 'absinthe fountain' — an ornate dome of silver and glass with spindly filigree taps shooting off from the sides. A sugar cube is placed on a perforated spoon above a tiny glass containing the lethal green liquid. Then the taps are used to gradually drizzle icy water over the sugar cube, sweetening the absinthe and giving it just the right amount of dilution, so it turns from a vicious-looking mouthwash to a more sophisticated, cloudy, pale green. I have to admit that, after several weeks in the fresh mountain air, nearly without a drop of alcohol, I was left slightly reeling and fuzzy around the edges in almost no time at all.

The morning of our departure from Antibes, we raced to catch the end of the covered market before we left for Nice. The

Cours Masséna in the heart of the town was packed with vendors and the stalls overflowed with fresh fruit, vegetables and flowers. We wandered happily among the fresh fish, the artichokes and piles of perfumed spices before heading along the coast to Nice, to this day one of my favourite journeys, which greeted us with blazing sunshine and seaside glamour.

It had been at least two hours since I'd last had some cheese, and my lactose senses were tingling. Lucky Jen was subsequently taken on a magical mystery tour through the labyrinthine cobbled streets of Vieux Nice in search of cheese. Well, nothing new for her there, really, and she did get an ice cream for her patience.

The rest of the afternoon was spent with small hockey-puck-sized discs of tangy goat's cheese, cold beer and slices of delicious smoked ham from the market, sliced decadently thick, while sitting on the pebble beach and skimming stones into the clear, blue sea. Heaven.

★ ★ ★

After waving a slightly sunburned Jen off at the airport, I took that same winding bus journey back to Grasse. The anxiety I felt on my first journey had been completely replaced by a desire to get back into the mix, to make sure that I made the most of my remaining time with the girls and learned as much as I could before heading back to the grind in London. From Grasse, I took another small bus to the foot of the mountain and commenced the walk up to the farm. I didn't want to bother Bruno asking for a lift and it was a great day for a walk.

Despite the heat and the heavy rucksack, there was a spring in my step as I made my way up the winding pathway. My eye was on my watch, knowing that on a day like this Julien would surely be out with the herd. My ears strained to hear the clanking of goat bells in the distance, like a call to prayer.

I met them about twenty minutes from the farmhouse at one of their favourite dining spots. The road cut through a small, flat piece of land, clear of trees with the exception of those lining the perilous scraggy drop down the mountain. The herbs and grasses here were to the ladies' taste; the trees provided cool shade and tasty leaves, and the rocky outcrops were sufficiently precarious to be just perfect for clambering over to survey the world below.

Several goat couples were playing the head-butting game as I arrived. Two goats vying for an upgrade on the social pecking order will stand off against each other before rearing up on their hind legs in unison and crashing their heads together. Thankfully, their thick skulls are evolutionarily well padded and there seems to be little lasting damage, other than that done to their pride.

I caught up with Julien about the week's activities, such as the quantity of milk produced and the quality of the cheeses. The remaining expectant mothers had now all given birth and there were a few new faces in the children's pen. There had also sadly been a death: one of the adult male goats had passed away. We weren't quite sure why, and Bruno's answers weren't exactly forthcoming. It's just one of those sad facts of farm life. Dusty and sweaty, we slowly made our way back to the farm and, although the sky was still blue and cloudless, I felt a fleeting grey shadow pass over me at the thought of leaving this behind for suits and commutes back home.

That evening was a real treat. I'd managed to track down a pretty reasonable piece of Stilton, some well-aged Comté for Julien (who talked at length about how much he loved the stuff, often with a slightly crazed look in his eyes) and a bottle of red that I remembered from my days in Aix. I shared them with Bruno and Julien, and, while there were the inevitable complaints that I had not only brought a cow's-milk cheese to the table, but an English one at that, the Stilton vanished very quickly.

* * *

My last few days on the farm were excellent, and I spent as much time as possible with the adult goats and the kids, the youngest of whom I'd had a hand in naming. Gadget and Gremlin were two of my favourites — cheeky little beggars who would jump and clamber all over me as soon as I entered the shed, nibbling at me gently with their sharp little teeth.

Tourists had started making their way up the mountain paths, and we had a number of visitors to the farm. I was more than happy to be giving tours in English (something of a relief from the solid French that I was speaking). The weather had also warmed up sufficiently for us to eat outside. With local produce, fine fresh cheeses and stunning views, it made for lunchtime perfection, hampered only by the occasional curious goat on the picnic table, trying to pick through the contents of our salad bowl.

But within no time at all I was packing my

bags, preparing to head down the mountain one final time. Julien had arranged to stay longer and I found myself wishing that I could do the same. I was even sad to be leaving the trailer behind: her sun-bleached colours and wiring idiosyncrasies had grown on me.

The goats had a new WWOOFer coming to replace me in a few days' time and they would get on just fine. They were stubborn (you won't know the true extent of this until you have pushed an overweight and matronly goat up a mountain through a dense wood — thanks for the memories, Tamtam) but magnificent, and I was leaving immeasurably richer than when I arrived. I was also a full stone lighter and had a reasonably impressive beard.

★　★　★

From my time on the farm, my knowledge of cheese making had exploded and eventually I think I managed not to be too much of an embarrassment to Bruno, although I would not dream of describing myself as adept at the goat-farming life. I tried hard, put in the hours and enjoyed the work, but it was clear that I was out of touch with physical, practical work and generally getting my hands dirty. There was very little call for spread-sheets on this mountain.

An area that I found particularly challenging during my stay was the milking room. It had a fair amount of equipment designed to receive the milk and to help keep it cool and hygienic. The numerous pipes, valves and filters required cleaning on a regular basis — a complicated process of turning this valve, pressing that button, leaving this hose here and mopping up that puddle of milk there. There were instructions for this process, in French of course, designed to be simple enough for an English accountant to understand. Over time I was left with an increasing degree of responsibility and, generally speaking, I wasn't terrible at it.

However, I do have the vivid memory of an event that to this day makes me want to curl up in embarrassment. We had finished milking and the milk had been transferred to the *fromagerie*. I was left in charge of the cleaning and had been following the instructions carefully: turning this lever, pressing that button, all was going swimmingly.

However, at one point when cleaning out the large milk vat, I had misunderstood that I was meant to trap the powerful hot-water hose under the heavy lid of the vat and had instead left it under a flimsy plastic one that fills a small opening that allows you to see in when the big lid is down. The result of putting high pressure through the hose was, I can only infer from the aftermath, akin to the classic cartoon image of a fireman's hose gone rogue. Upon discovering my mistake I felt sheepish, apologized, and swept out the water.

It wasn't until later that evening, when the milking had finished and the milk was in the tank, that Bruno spotted a problem. The motor that turned the milk to make sure that it chilled and developed evenly had stopped working, as it was waterlogged.

I wasn't aware of this and was warm and comfortable in the house, enjoying a well-intentioned but somewhat unfortunately executed 'traditional British' meal I had cooked for everyone. It turns out that goat milk just doesn't make for a particularly pleasant or satisfying custard. I asked Julien where Bruno was, as I hadn't seen him for a while, not having taken part in the evening milking. Julien mentioned that there was a problem in the milking room. 'Something to do with the motor being full of water', he said with his mouth full. Feeling guilty, I walked down to the milking room in the pitch-black night. There was a light on, and I could hear a familiar whirring sound that seemed out of place.

I didn't go in, I didn't say anything, I just turned around and walked back to the house in shame. The lonesome sound of that hairdryer in the dark still haunts me to this day.

★   ★   ★

Working on the farm taught me a huge amount and helped me overcome some of my innate clumsiness, but one of the things it really brought to my attention was a serious point that, as a consumer, I hadn't previously given sufficient consideration. Essentially, at the centre of the dairy industry lies the uncomfortable image of a mother separated from her child.

A baby animal might be the cutest thing in the world but, if left to natural order, it will damage the profitability of the farm. Leaving a baby goat to feed from its mother, no matter how natural and right that might seem to be, reduces the quantity of the milk that can be used to make cheese.

Additionally, infant males will never be able to contribute to milk production and, while a troop will have some males, they are often supplied from other breeding stock to help keep the gene pool deep. Young males are a heavy cost for the farm to support, not even taking into consideration the careful treatment and handling that they require to prevent damage caused by their sometimes aggressive behaviour.

Making cheese is an activity with precious little margin in it at the best of times and, sadly, unchecked sentimentality — particularly in relation to the two points just mentioned — can make the difference between a viable business and a failing one.

During my time on the farm, I separated young goats from their mothers as soon as they were old enough to feed alone, and I saw the truck take away the young males on an all-too-regular basis. I did not enjoy this, but it was important to have had the opportunity to see it at first hand, and I feel that it has given me an increased appreciation for the providers of the cheeses that we love, be they human or animal.

I should point out here that I am a meat eater. I'm not proud of it, and maybe one day I will become vegetarian, although I find it hard to see that happening in the near future. I'm not going to justify my choice to eat meat. I'm not sure that it is particularly defensible. But as a consumer I do get to vote with my income as to how the animals that ultimately feed me are cared for before they end up on my plate. This is not a responsibility to be taken lightly, particularly when we consider outrages such as the horsemeat scandal that was big news in early 2013 as I started writing this book.

Back on the farm, the male baby goats may have a short life, but at the very least it's a rich one. They see little suffering and do much frolicking. Sadly, the artificial shortening of their life is necessary to keep the farm profitable, which in turn supports the wonderful lifestyle of the whole herd, and adds richness and variety to the region.

In truth, however, my convictions did not always help in making the all-too-regular evening meal of goat sausages easy to swallow.

★ ★ ★

On the day I left Bruno's, there's no doubt I was sad to be leaving. However, it turned out that I was not leaving the farm empty-handed. Those generous goats gave me a parting present that I wouldn't forget in a while.

There's no easy way to put this. Sometimes goats have fleas. These goats had fleas and, as a consequence, the farm had fleas. Yes, you could wash your clothes, but as soon as you put new ones on and stood near a goat, they would jump all over you. I had a lot of bites around my ankles and along my waistband, which itched enormously.

Naïvely, I thought that when I got back to London I would be able to wash everything that I wanted to keep and bin the clothing that was frankly too goaty for city life. After a week or so of relative peace, the bites started again and it was clear I had infested both the London flat and Jen, who had not come within miles of a goat, with fleas. As you might imagine, I was not wildly popular when we discovered this. Fortunately for me, there are some excellent products available for dealing with the problem (and, as it turns out, the ladybird infestation that we didn't know we had), but that doesn't alleviate the shame of it.

★ ★ ★

Back in London the itch of the goat fleas had subsided. I'd been bitten by a different sort of bug. It was hard to express but essentially boiled down to the need for a significant and lasting change in my life.

I had nothing against my work at the NAO: it was comfortable, well paid and stretched me sufficiently, mentally speaking. There were some at the office who had spent their entire working lives there; that was their decision and I respected and understood that. As I said, it can be a comfortable place of employment. But that was just what I was trying to get away from. I felt that I was in the process of settling down, growing some serious roots.

I was in a rut, a comfortable, pleasant and well-furnished rut. The danger was that, if I didn't do something now, I would stay there for ever, in a happy but monotonous routine of work, sleep, socializing, the occasional disastrous kitchen experiment and endless repeats of *Top Gear*.

I came back from France motivated and excited, something that I hadn't felt for a few years. My insight from working on the farm had opened windows into this strange new world. I felt as if I had only just scratched the surface, that there was so much more to this industry than I had ever really imagined. I was ravenous for any snippet of useful information, cheese recipes, cheese histories, unexplored London cheese shops.

Our bookshelves suddenly blossomed with cheese-themed books, and the fridge became even fuller of interesting odds and ends of the yellow stuff. I had learned that cheese is fascinating; it is an expression of the landscape, the breeding and good husbandry of animals, the social history of the region and even the rise and fall of nations and empires. It is all too easy to ignore, when presented with a cheese board, the origins of the cheeses before us; but, in my opinion, understanding the why, where, how and by whom of cheese makes the tasting all the more significant.

The evolutionary pressure on cheese is fierce: if a cheese recipe is consistently unpopular, the producer will quickly stop making it. There are many who make cheese and even more who *have made* cheese. The successes are passed on and the failures weeded out by consumer selection such that the cheeses we have today are finely honed, lean and ready for your enjoyment.

Often, cheeses arrived to meet a local need that can seem archaic to us with our easily obtainable international cheese-boards. For example the reason for making huge, cooked Alpine cheeses was to preserve, through the winter, the high quality of milk given by cows grazing on the luscious grass in Alpine pastures. This kind of pressure simply didn't exist in the more temperate south-west France, where the rocky landscape was more suited to sheep than cows, and consequently blue ewe's milk cheeses such as Roquefort came into being. The south-east and central regions of France are replete with goats, the skill for their husbandry left by the Moors in their movement across Europe.

Over centuries, breeds were carefully selected and recipes adjusted. The traditional cheeses are each worthy of a book, and the depth of human interest is enormous. But I also found out, a little to my shock, that I had entered the world of cheese during a difficult time. This fascinating link between cheese and human history is, as you are reading this very sentence, being dangerously eroded. The mass-produced industrial cheeses that line our supermarket shelves may bear the name of their ancestors, but they are not the same. They look similar and often taste pleasant, they are undoubtedly technologically brilliant and above all cheap, but they are not the same, they don't have the same pedigree.

In addition to the rise of industrialization and commoditization of our food chain, increased social mobility has provided futures for the children of farmers that appear significantly more appealing than life at the dairy. There are many examples of cheeses in France that are on the verge of being lost as no one is willing to take up the reins of the now ageing experts.

From working with Bruno, Françoise and

Julien, and from my research, I had come to realize that the people who work in cheese are incredibly interesting. It's another kind of natural selection in a way. There is no money in cheese, at least not in artisanal and farmhouse cheese. The independent and highly skilled jobs of the farmer, the cheese maker, the *affineur* (the person responsible for the *affinage*, or the maturing and refining, of the cheese) and the cheesemonger all require remuneration. Given that it's difficult to sell a cheese for a lot of money (certainly when it starts becoming more expensive than top-end cuts of meat) it is hard to provide each of the individuals working along the supply chain with a margin that sufficiently represents their efforts.

So why then do people make cheese, age cheese and sell cheese? The reasons are complex and numerous and, importantly, more interesting than simply making money. I'm not saying that I'm against doing something profitable in principle, just that the people who choose not to tend to have some interesting things to say.

I had returned to London a cheese evangelist, happy to bore the hind legs off anyone foolish to stand before me. The big question now, though, was: what next?

6

Decision Time

How was I ever going to settle back into the city routine after such an eye-opening experience? At the time it didn't seem possible, yet all it took was a few weeks.

After the initial excitement of the flea and ladybird infestations, the boiler breakdown and the overly active mice that we shared our flat with, the routine of daily London life quickly reasserted itself.

Shiny shoes replaced walking boots, suit and tie replaced farm clothes and a slightly nicked and pasty face replaced the patchy beard that I had been working so hard on. My Oyster card was renewed and, before you could say 'International Financial Reporting Standards', I was back in the office in front of my computer. With the exception of a very full inbox, things were largely as I had left them.

It was good to be back and see work colleagues and friends again, and they were to some degree interested in what I'd been up to and why I hadn't brought them back any cheese (fresh goat's cheese really doesn't travel very well — a sad truth). Most importantly, they wanted to know if I still smelled as much like a goat as Jen had been saying I did.

On that score there was some improvement: a number of items of clothing had been deemed irredeemable and binned and I had taken many, many showers. But I still had work to do.

* * *

In government accounting, a 31 March year end is the norm, so our clients tended to prepare their accounts in April ready for submission to us in late May or early June. We, as auditors, would then review them such that we can give our OK to their publication before Parliament takes its summer recess in July. Because all the accounts have the same deadline (and there are a large number of them: approximately five hundred covering almost the entirety of central-government spending) a lot of planning is required to make sure that the busy period is as efficient as possible.

I got stuck in and projects, as they do, quickly overtook me. Before long I was back in Swindon for the final audit season. Not that this was a particularly bad thing, though — of course it was a shame not to be with Jen during the week (despite the rumours that she had been spreading about my caprine aroma), but there were lots of interesting problems to be solved and publication dates to be met. On top of this, as a newly qualified accountant, I had some real responsibilities now.

There was one significant problem, though. Swindon was not well served for cheese shops, which was pretty frustrating. I had a real craving for decent cheese, and in the beautiful countryside that surrounded the city I was sure that there were lovely things being made, but how to find them? Of course, there were supermarkets, but supermarkets are to cheese what supermarkets are to, well, just about everything, really. Of course, I still use them — it's difficult not to — but I always feel bad about it afterwards, particularly if there are other, better options.

I'm not professing to be an expert here — my interest and experience lie in a small corner of the food industry — but what I've seen seems to tally well with what I've heard in the media generally about other produce found in supermarkets, particularly meat.

Now I know that there are exceptions, particularly in France, where some small producers feed into local supermarkets, but in my opinion you shouldn't really expect to be able to find 'good' cheese in a supermarket. Any supplier capable of producing the necessary quantity of homogeneous cheese to supply a national supermarket chain is almost certainly going to be industrial in nature. Bruno, with his beautiful herd of eighty goats, would certainly never have been able to produce enough cheese to become a national supplier, meaning that, if you limit yourself to buying cheese from a supermarket, you will never taste the product that he and many others like him have so painstakingly and lovingly created.

So what do I mean by 'good' cheese? I mean cheese with character, mostly raw-milk cheeses, made with traditional techniques and a firm link to the animals that produced the milk. These cheeses change with the seasons, with the weather and with the mood of the livestock. They are an almost living expression of their *terroir* — their geographical area with its unique characteristics — and they are fascinating.

Raw milk is milk that hasn't been subjected to heat treatment for pasteurization purposes. This is important because the act of pasteurization essentially kills the living microbial flora that connect the cheese to its environment; it kills a significant part of the cheese's personality. The problem, however, is that raw milk is variable, unpredictable and expensive — generally requiring extra testing before getting to market. For these reasons many, or even most, of the cheeses found in a supermarket, because they are produced on a large scale, are pasteurized.

You can make cheese to a recipe and it might taste nice — you can do it in your kitchen, in fact — but, if you're buying in your milk from an unknown dairy, where the diet and grazing habits of the herd are unknown to you, then you tend to question the validity of the exercise. Certainly, I do. For me, a good cheese has character, and here I don't just mean in its flavour, but also moral character. As I said, a good cheese is an expression of its *terroir*, of the farmer and his herd, of social history and economics. A good cheese doesn't have to have been around for a long time, but you will often find the old ones are good, thanks to economic and gustative natural selection.

Most likely, in the supermarket you won't find small farmhouse productions or artisans that have carefully selected their milk — although this may well be the image presented to you on the packaging. And, really, if a supermarket did have a source of good cheese, you should ask yourself whether they would have the know-how to properly care for it, the training to spot and rectify problems in maturing it and, importantly, the link with the producer. I don't doubt that there are some great products and great people working in the supermarket cheese sector, but, since I had seen the other side with Bruno and the effort required in making and marketing a cheese, I've rarely walked away from a supermarket cheese purchase feeling happy about the transaction.

There's no question for me: anyone interested enough in cheese to have bought this book should be investing a little bit of time in building up a relationship with a cheesemonger. They will give you the advice that you need regarding what's good now, where it came from and how best to enjoy it.

You vote for the future with your wallet or purse; please vote for a future where real cheese is bought and sold in cheese shops and markets or direct from the farm, by trained professionals dedicated to supporting honest, traditional (or even not so traditional) producers, who focus on quality rather than mass production. It may be a bit more expensive, but the richness and opportunity to be part of the story around a good cheese more than amply make up the difference.

★ ★ ★

My time in the cheese desert of Swindon during the week left me hungry for London curd-exploration trips at the weekend, and, fortunately, there was plenty on offer. A great first stop was the exquisitely detailed and laid-out La Fromagerie in London's Marylebone, complete with its own walk-in cheese room, dark and wonderfully fragrant, with shelves heaving under the weight of beautifully presented cheeses.

Patricia Michelson, the creator of the shop, is a bit of a personal hero to me, and I don't doubt for a minute that her awesomely inspirational book, *The Cheese Room*, was one of the factors that pushed me into my future career change. Jen had given it to me as a gift on our first Valentine's Day.

In terms of shop layout, however, my firm favourite was Neal's Yard Dairy at London Bridge. It feels very much that the design — functional, not particularly warm, and fairly humid — was created with the well-being of the cheese at the forefront of everyone's mind. Considerations of the client were secondary, in design at least, although the staff are warm and friendly and exceedingly knowledgeable, so playing second fiddle to the cheeses doesn't ever feel like too much of a hardship.

Cheese is used as decoration, with all manner of wonderful things lining the walls; this, of course, is made possible by the ambient conditions.

I loved the method they used to sell: basically the tried-and-tested 'if they taste it, they'll buy it,' and, really, who doesn't like being offered lots of cheese to taste? But where the Neal's Yard sellers differ is that, rather than just offering, they would try the cheese with you, commenting on it, putting words to the flavours and sensations, and essentially giving you a mini tasting class. This is fun to be on the receiving end of, and I can imagine is outrageously successful; it certainly has been with me.

While I was in the area of London Bridge, though, I would always take a wander through Borough Market, perhaps London's glossiest food destination. There would always be plenty to be excited about as I fought my way through the throng, but, when I was looking for some French cheeses to complement the UK offerings from Neal's Yard, there was a small stall that I would find myself often gravitating towards. They didn't have a huge selection of cheese, but, as you walked past, they were often ready to give you a taste. I had a bit of a thing for their Perail.

It's a flat white disc with a bloomy rind that ages to an off-white yellow. It's quite unusual in French cheeses in that it's a creamy ewe's-milk cheese. It comes from the same region as Roquefort (using milk from the same race of ewe, the Lacaune), in the Midi-Pyrénées in southern France. It has a strong, farmyard, animal flavour with a beautiful, creamy centre that caresses the tongue yet manages not to be cloying. The raw milk gives a long woolly finish, which with age can get really quite punchy. A delight.

⋆ ⋆ ⋆

Another piece of good news was the excellent progress that Jen was making in learning to like cheese.

Now I realize that that particular comment makes me sound like the kind of cheese bore who would be unbearable to live with. To be honest, there's probably a grain of truth in that: I wouldn't say that our relationship couldn't have survived a penchant for Stilton with apricots in it, but I'm glad we didn't have to put it to the test.

Jen has a great palate and a brilliant knack for putting words to flavours. Sometimes she hid her inward sighs well on discovering that I had bought yet more cheese, sometimes less so; but, when it came down to it, she was always game to analyse a new arrival, which made exploring the cheeses that London had made available all the more enjoyable.

While cheese was certainly always on my radar, I should add that it wasn't just the delights of *fromage* that I was lusting after on those weekend visits. It was good food in general.

Jen and I did a lot of cooking and the occasional restaurant review; we followed food trends and tried out up-and-comers on the London restaurant scene; we even set up our own food blog. We cared about exploring food culture and invested time and money in it. I had a pet yeast starter in the fridge, and Jen often had flour in her hair as a result of her latest baking experiment.

As time went on, I was starting to have serious questions about whether my cheese involvement should remain on an enthusiastic hobbyist level, or whether I should be looking at taking this interest more seriously.

★   ★   ★

Food had been creeping into ever more aspects of our lives, and it had already influenced a number of our holiday choices.

Visits to the village of Cheddar in Somerset and the hot, beautiful and wine-saturated Saint-Émilion near Bordeaux in France were good examples. But perhaps the most 'out there' destination (really rather masochistic in retrospect) was our camping visit to Islay.

Islay (pronounced Eye-luh) is a small Southern Hebridean Scottish island that houses many of the big names in Scottish peaty whiskies. We had to decide to camp, to wild-camp, actually, which was a brave move for Jen, given that she had never really been in a tent before and that the Southern Hebrides are not renowned for their clement weather.

It rained a lot, we got eaten alive by midges, we ate a lot of beautifully fresh seafood and we drank a lot of spectacular whisky. It must be said, the day we spent at the Laphroaig distillery was one of the best of my life. The sun came out and we spent nine hours in glorious coastal surroundings tasting different vintages and learning about the distilling and production. It was my equivalent of a chocolate factory or Disney World.

These holidays were great but again, before long, we were back in the same routine. It's difficult to explain, but we were still in what I considered to be this comfortable rut — a pleasant enough existence with sufficient salary for our needs and probably our own property within a couple of years. We had friends, family and a perfectly agreeable lifestyle. The problem was that it was all we had really known. There was this nagging feeling that we might be missing out on something huge. We really didn't know what that might be, just that, if we didn't take the leap now, we almost certainly never would.

I can't profess to speak for Jen on this, but the fundamental issue that I was trying to address was that I didn't want to grow old having only ever seen the inside of one office; I didn't want to have regrets about not trying to chase down my dreams; and I wanted to make sure that I got the most out of my time with Jen in the 'pre-family' era of our relationship.

I think that the idea that if we were to do something different we might move to France had always been a strong possibility. You already know that I was infatuated with the place, and Jen wasn't too far behind me. She had studied modern languages at university and had spent a year living and working in Paris. She had found Paris a rather intimidating city, no thanks to the oppressive cupboard of an apartment that she had rented, but she was very keen to go back and try France again, now that she was a bit more worldly-wise.

We established that we were both keen to try to fully immerse ourselves in both the food culture and the language of France. What we were after was an experiment, a test to see whether we really wanted to be living as we were in London. We decided that, if we spent two years in another country (France), that would be long enough for the novelty to wear off. We would be subjected to the humdrum, the bureaucracy, the taxes, the shopping for toothpaste.

It's hard to say exactly when we decided concretely that we would move to France, but I believe that it was during the week between Christmas and New Year's Eve at the end of 2010. We had reached a position where we had talked about it enough to know that we had to try it, or we would regret it for ever, so we made a pact (after a night out in a Clapham pub). We would not renew our rental lease when it came to an end in August 2011; we would not look for another apartment in London.

We both knew at that point that this would happen; there was a finality to it. In the meantime there were some serious details to work out. Not least, how we were going to support ourselves out there. We had some money saved up but that wouldn't last too long — Jen would have to go freelance, and I would have to find paying work, if I could. How I would go about finding a job in France, and, more specifically, in cheese, I had no idea, but I was excited by the prospect of it.

★ ★ ★

I had always been aware that the office offered career breaks, but it had never previously occurred to me that I might take one. This, however, was perfect — a trial separation from accountancy and the opportunity to dip a toe in the cheesy waters before leaving the suit and calculator at the side of the pool and diving in head first.

The real upside was that, if we crashed and burned in France, I could call the break off early and be resettled and earning again in fairly short order. I really didn't think that we would need that option, but having it would make the risk somewhat easier to take.

During this mulling-over period, which actually lasted for a couple of months as we slowly brought our ideas into line, I found myself engaging in genuine 'double think' at work, planning for future events and audit cycles, while at the same time knowing with certainty that I wouldn't be there. I never lied outright, but I suppose at times, mainly through omission, I gave a misleading indication that I would still be in the office in eight months' time.

As I sat looking at my 'Business Case for Career Break' document, deciding whether this was really the direction that I wanted to take, all I could see was a fuzzy wish to pursue a career in the French cheese industry. The potential benefits that I had listed rang a little hollow: foreign-language skills were not wildly useful in government auditing, and understanding how other workplaces function would have little relevance, since we audited relatively few farms and cheese shops.

I was mentally preparing myself to be laughed out of the room. But that was OK: I was certain that, whether the career break application was accepted or not, I would be leaving London, and I would quit the NAO if necessary.

To my surprise, just a week later, my application was returned, approved. It was all systems go!

7

A Reconnaissance Mission

People have often asked me what made us pick Lyon, but in truth there was no one single reason.

Paris had been counted out quite early on in our thinking. Jen had lived in the capital a few years previously for her year abroad while she was at Cambridge, and was keen to experience somewhere new, and, to be honest, after several visits to Paris, I hadn't felt the pull of the city that so many write, sing and romanticize about. It always seemed to be teetering on the edge of something ever so slightly frenzied, lots of hurried footsteps, downturned glances and icily stylish people. It never seemed to smell particularly nice, either.

We wanted something that was just a little bit less frenetic and a little bit warmer around the edges. I had travelled through Lyon once several years ago, stopping for a night at a really rather glamorous youth hostel in the old part of town on my way to Marseille and on to Spain while InterRailing. I had recollections of rivers, open squares, a long cobbled street of restaurants festooned with coloured lights and thrumming with chatter, and the tall Basilique de Fourvière, perched on the hill overlooking the city. That night I'd made my way back from a smoky café to the hostel and there was a point on one of the bridges where the basilica and the biscuit-coloured cathedral in the old town were perfectly in line, lit up in the dark with a friendly orange hue. I remember being struck then by how beautiful this city was. I hadn't been expecting that: Lyon had always been little more than a thoroughfare for winter tourists on their way to the pistes of the Alps as far as I was concerned, rather than a destination in its own right. I remember feeling annoyed with myself then that I hadn't planned to stay longer than that one evening, and the more I thought about it, the more Lyon became a definite contender for our future home.

Jen had never been there, and, while she said she was pretty happy to trust my judgement (I did genuinely think she would like it), I didn't feel comfortable about her making such a big decision blind, so we decided to spend a few days' holiday there in late spring 2011 — a reconnaissance mission to see how good a fit it might prove to be for us and our French adventure.

While I'm generally content to play things by ear and go with the flow, Jen tends to function on a slightly more military scale of organization, so we arrived at the airport with a sheaf of lists and ideas for itineraries. She had found us a little studio to rent for the week, with a small kitchen so we wouldn't be completely reliant on restaurant meals. As undeniably practical as this was, I did wonder whether we would both get sucked into the creamy centre of Lyon as France's capital of gastronomy, and find ourselves stumbling out of restaurants each night anyway, full of pork products and rich sauces and wine that smelled faintly of blackberries.

We arrived late on a Friday evening, both of us having come straight from our respective offices. Weeks before holidays are usually the hardest, and this was no exception: we were exhausted and did nothing more than track down our little studio, which was in Vaise — an almost-suburb at the end of one of the Métro lines — and flop into bed.

The next morning, we both agreed that the famous Les Halles de Lyon Paul Bocuse — Lyon's covered market that was fêted as a must-see foodie destination — would be first on our list of things to do.

I'm not sure what Jen was expecting, but I had certainly imagined that this temple to gastronomy and the finest of French produce would be housed in the centre of town, on the grand and elegant Presqu'île (literally the 'almost island') that falls between the two rivers. I had pictured a domed glass roof, the odd marble column and no small amount of pomp. Perhaps there would even be a statue of the great man himself — Paul Bocuse — smiling benevolently down at the stallholders and market traders like a deity in a chef's hat.

We were scrutinizing the map, feeling certain that we'd gone wrong somewhere as we arrived in front of Les Halles. The building that greeted us was in the 3rd arrondissement — a newer, duller part of town with few Métro stations and even less charm. It was a squat glass box of a thing, sandwiched between a frozen-food store and a pharmacy, and cowering in the shadow of an enormous and spectacularly ugly multistorey car park. It all looked pretty grim.

As we entered, though, our fears very quickly vanished. Rows upon rows of stalls piled high with beautiful produce beckoned to us and we wandered among them slowly, exclaiming at the punnets of the year's first wild strawberries, the blurring steel of the butcher's knives as they minced beef by hand for a customer's steak-tartare dinner party, the bright-eyed fish and juicy-looking scallops on ice at the fishmonger's, and, of course, the cheese!

Along one side of the building were several small restaurants, where families and off-duty traders were enjoying lunch. Waiters shouted to clear a path as they brought trays of oysters and carafes of white wine, little dishes of crunchy pork scratchings, crispily coated *andouillettes* (a kind of coarse-grained sausage traditionally made from pig's intestines) and dishes of creamy *gratin dauphinois* (a very rich dish of finely sliced potatoes and a lot of cheese and cream). Kids as young as three or four were attacking plates of langoustines with a dexterity and relish that left me open-mouthed. My childhood self would have shuddered at even the thought of eating any seafood more exotic than a fish finger.

After we'd circled back around to the entrance, the cheese stalls were calling to me, and I could see that Jen had the jewel-coloured *pâtisseries* in her sights. We went our separate ways, promising to meet up later without having bankrupted ourselves. I prepared myself for a cheese tour.

The sellers here were seriously impressive. I loitered by one stall in the centre of the market and watched them for a while. There was a ticketing system at work here, and customers queued noisily, waiting for their numbers to be called. The stall was laid out in a horseshoe shape, and there was something familiar about the logo on the signs, but I couldn't quite put my finger on what it was. Grabbing a ticket, I shamelessly eavesdropped on the customers in front of me as they had their requests met. The guy behind the counter was in his forties, with greying hair, glasses and a kindly face. I wondered if this was the Etienne Boissy mentioned on the sign. I came away with a brown paper bag containing a sizeable chunk of Roquefort, and a small creamy goat's cheese that apparently had been made by monks who infused thyme into the milk to give a subtle herby aftertaste. I had been assured that these would be perfect for a picnic lunch.

Jen and I headed for the park, and indulged in what is possibly the most unhealthy picnic of all time, consisting of a lot of cheese and even more macaroons. Jen had been unable to resist the plethora of flavours on offer and had come away with an enormous bagful and a sheepish expression. As we lay back on the grass in the sunshine feeling almost painfully full, Jen, laughing, described Les Halles as being 'Like Borough Market's sexier French cousin'.

I sat up. That's where I'd seen the logo before. The shop in Les Halles, Mons, had a branch at Borough in London. In fact, it was the stall that I had frequently visited for its delicious Perail. I explained this to Jen and we grinned at each other. Lyon was looking more and more promising.

The rest of our reconnaissance trip was spent being unashamedly touristy. We drank beers on a barge by the river, warmed up our rusty French on long-suffering waiters, trekked up the hill in the blazing sunshine to the basilica (which was actually all a bit gold-plated and oppressive) and the view it commanded (which was wonderful), and mooched around the cobbled streets of the old part of town, taking copious photographs and imagining ourselves living there.

★　★　★

Lyon hadn't disappointed us, and I was really pleased that Jen was as excited about the prospect of living there as I was. As we touched down in London, it was as if our plan had become something a lot more tangible and neither of us wanted to turn back.

I found that I couldn't get the Mons connection out of my head, and images of me behind that horseshoe-shaped glass counter, confidently advising the great and the good of Lyon on their cheesy choices kept resurfacing. The Saturday after we got back, I went to Borough Market and made a beeline for the Mons stall.

The market was fairly quiet, and at the stall there was a large platter covered in small cubes of aged, buttery Comté laid out at the front for passers-by to taste. As I approached, I was conscious of quite how ludicrous I might be about to sound. I just hoped they wouldn't laugh me out of the market.

'Hi, there. Umm . . . I wonder if you can help me,' I said to one of the guys behind the stall, sounding as if I were on the phone to a customer-services call centre somewhere. 'I was wondering if it would be possible to get some work experience with you guys out in France.'

'Oh, sure, OK,' he said, with only a hint of surprise. 'Are you in the food industry, then?'

'No, I'm a . . . no. I'm not.'

A look passed between him and the other guy manning the stall, and he hid a smile behind his hand. 'Here you go,' he said, passing me a business card. 'This is the guy you need to get in touch with — maybe he'll be able to help.'

The name on the card said Jon Thrupp, and just a couple of days later we were meeting for a pint in a pub near London Bridge.

Jon was late. People working with the yellow stuff often are. Somehow, it seems to always want to suck you back in, just as you're trying to leave. I didn't begrudge him. I was so amazed that he was taking the time to actually meet with me. I mean, what could *he* possibly get out of this? That said, it was a little bit problematic as I wasn't 100 per cent sure that I would be able to recognize him. I was pretty sure that I had bought cheese from him before, but not certain.

After spending a while glancing at strangers and hoping for a glint of recognition, I was getting a little anxious about the whole thing. Then, in he walked. It was clearly the man. He just looked like the kind of guy who would be able to sell you shit-hot French cheese on a market stall. I think it had something to do with the beard.

Over a solid pint (or several) of bitter, I explained to Jon my goal of entering the French cheese industry and getting a real flavour of how it all worked over there. I explained that we would be living in Lyon and how I'd seen the shop in Les Halles. In retrospect, I probably wasn't particularly coherent, but Jon understood immediately what I needed: an overview of the industry and some contacts to get me started.

Jon had started his cheese career path in the early days of Neal's Yard Dairy. He came into contact with Hervé Mons, the co-founder of the Mons family business, and left Neal's Yard to train with Hervé in the caves at Roanne. Jon went on to become the director of Mons UK and now receives deliveries from Hervé every week to sell at the Borough Market stall and a number of restaurants and other shops.

Each phrase emanated passion and conviction and I was hanging on every word. He did have a habit of dropping names into conversations in such a way that I felt I really ought to have recognized them — clearly, I had a fair amount of research to do.

Nod and smile, ask leading questions . . .

According to Jon, to understand the cheese world, you have to have experienced production, *affinage*, retail and wholesale. One of the great things about the Mons organization was that it gave relatively easy access to all of these operations. *Affinage* and wholesale took place in the caves at Roanne (not far from Lyon), retail in the shops such as the shop that we'd seen in Lyon, and, as for the production, well, Hervé Mons had all the contacts that one could ever need.

Though never effusive, Jon clearly cared deeply about Hervé and his company and it was infectious. I realized that if I played my cards right, and I could persuade this Hervé to take a chance on me, I might be able to achieve everything that I was hoping for with my career break. What was more, the fact that Jon had trained with him already was a great precedent, showing that they had taken on an Englishman — I really had no idea whether the doors would be firmly closed to 'foreigners'.

We finished up our drinks and left the pub, Jon promising that he would put in a good word for me with Hervé and would pass on the relevant contact details. I left feeling a lot closer to understanding what I wanted to achieve and what seemed like a fairly direct, although not necessarily easy, path to how to achieve it.

★　★　★

Meanwhile, Jen had been busy house-hunting. We'd decided that Lyon was going to be our main base for our time in France, but we wanted to spend a bit of time exploring another area before we settled there. I've always felt that France is, much more so than England, a land made up of lots of different countries. As you drive across France, the changing landscapes are breathtaking: you can take in lavender fields, snow-capped mountains, rivers that twine through rocky gorges like blue ribbons, cobbled villages with chocolate-box cottages and rows and rows of sun-soaked vines in just a matter of hours. As we were due to be moving at the beginning of September, we decided to spend two months in south-west France, an area neither of us had explored before, to enjoy the last of the year's sunshine and get a feel for a different part of the country we both loved.

After several evenings browsing holiday lets and sabbatical homes, Jen had found us a small townhouse in the market town of Gaillac, which sits quietly halfway between Toulouse and Albi. It fitted all our criteria (good climate, accessible public transport, not in the middle of nowhere, affordable). The house was called L'Abeille, 'The Bee', and it looked beautiful but it wasn't available for the whole time we wanted it. The owners, Frankie and Nick, were keen walkers, and they also had a small, two-roomed flat on the ground floor of their own house, which they used as a hostel for passing pilgrims on the Santiago de Compostela trail. They agreed to let us stay in the hostel for the first two weeks, before we were able to move into L'Abeille. From the pictures she sent us, it looked basic but manageable, and there would be the prospect of sharing with any pilgrims who might pass by, but we were prepared to give it a try.

★ ★ ★

Before we knew it, it was August, and our house was a mess of packing boxes and parcel tape. We had our respective leaving parties at work, and organized a *bon voyage* meal for our friends at a little French bistro off Oxford Street. We'd been preparing for months, but it was really only as the wine glasses clinked in a toast that it clicked for me, and I could see the same expression of excitement and something a bit like fear on Jen's face at the other end of the table. *Oh, mon Dieu!* We were moving to France!

8

Sun, Wine and Bureaucracy

We quickly realized as we packed the car that it was going to be filled to the gunnels. So much so that I couldn't actually fit in the driver's seat. Poor Jen, who is, in her own words, five foot two on a good day, was therefore forced into the designated-driver role for our cross-country trip. Unfortunately for me, this also meant she had control of the music.

Despite the seemingly incessant Alanis Morissette blasting from the stereo, my spirits were really high. It felt liberating but very strange to be unemployed all of a sudden and, as we sped towards Gaillac and the unknown, I couldn't wait to start exploring the opportunities France had to offer.

As we headed south on the wide, and for the most part empty, roads, the sky got progressively more cloudless and became a deeper and deeper blue. We arrived in Gaillac as the sun was beginning to sink in the sky. The crumbling roofs of the townhouses glowed red in the golden light of the early evening, and, as we wound our way through the narrow streets to the Rue Grande Côte, where we would find the hostel, we could hear the thundering of the river over the weir.

Frankie was waiting on the front steps of the house to meet us. She was a petite redhead with sun-beaten skin and wrinkles around her eyes when she smiled, which she did often. Parking the heavily laden car on a road that was about as wide as a piece of string and on an incredibly steep angle was a bit of a mission, but, after several attempts, lots of air-traffic-control-style gesticulating from our new landlady and only one scrape against a wall, we triumphed and hopped out to meet her.

The hostel was tucked away behind the house that she shared with her partner, Nick — a rangy man with unruly grey hair and a wide selection of paint-splattered T-shirts. To access it, we walked down a narrow alleyway, which was strewn with sleepy cats, basking lazily in the sun and refusing to get out of our way as we passed. The hostel had two bedrooms, a bathroom and a communal living area with a basic gas-ring stove, a tiny sink and an even smaller fridge. It was decorated with obvious overspill items from the house above, and possibly from several previous houses. There were faded oil paintings on the walls, of fields and rivers all in varying shades of mustard, a pockmarked old pine table covered in a lace-doily-style cloth, a couple of lumpy old armchairs and an out-of-tune piano. It was clean and smelled of lemons.

As Frankie had said in her emails, it was pretty basic accommodation, but it would suit us just fine. The thick evening sunlight pouring in through the windows and pooling on the floor told us we probably wouldn't be spending too much time indoors, anyway.

For now, we had the hostel to ourselves. Frankie told us that there hadn't been many pilgrims passing through Gaillac this summer. She and Nick helped us to unpack our groaning little car, and then left us to get settled, telling us to come up to the house for a drink when we were done.

We spent the evening with Frankie, Nick, and a couple of their English friends who had a house in one of the picturesque walled villages, perched on a hill a little way upriver. We sat on their terrace, drinking citrusy wine, and then, as the air cooled, herbal tea made with lemon verbena from their impressive herb garden. They told us about the area, and the places that were worth exploring. While I was met with fairly blank looks when I asked about any known cheese producers in the area, we did find out about some châteaux and other winemakers who were worth a visit, as well as some beautiful wild swimming spots and fortified towns.

The following day, we explored the town. It had an air of crumbling elegance about it. The masterpiece was a redbrick abbey with pepper-pot towers and beautifully manicured gardens, which stretched along the banks of the river. It sat like a sentinel just at the entrance to the town. The main square was well kempt and neatly paved, surrounded by cafés and a few small restaurants, and with a fountain at its centre.

We found a smaller, cobbled and slightly more dilapidated square closer to the hostel, which hosted a market twice weekly. Dough-nut peaches and pumpkins vied for space with apples from the local orchard and pots and pots of thick, golden honey. Sadly, there really was no local cheese to be found, the farmers attending the market having travelled almost a hundred kilometres to show their, albeit delicious, wares.

We quickly settled into a routine. Jen was working three or four days a week for those two months in Gaillac, and would be going back to full-time work once we arrived in Lyon. Each morning, she would set up a small table and folding chair outside the hostel, in the sunlit alley, and would crack on with work while I went off with my camera, visiting local food producers, hiking along the river or driving out to one of the neighbouring towns. On her days off, we'd go exploring together. Taking a drive out of town, we'd take it in turns to be designated driver, and find a couple of winemakers to go and see. This needed very little research, as the area was positively teeming with vineyards, and you had to venture only a couple of kilometres out of the town before the signs for 'Ventes et Dégustations' (sales and tastings) would start springing up along the side of the road.

We went on several of these excursions during our time in Gaillac, but we certainly had a favourite that saw a fair amount of our repeat business. The producers in question are known as Château Bouscaillous. Their tasting room, lined with rustic displays of bottles and wine paraphernalia, had several upturned barrels functioning as tables, with bar stools around them. It was clearly designed to accommodate great coachloads of tourists when necessary, but, when only small groups were present, the warmth of the welcome was unparalleled.

Gaillac as a wine-producing area was interesting in that a large number of different styles of wine were permitted, from traditional reds, rosés and whites (sweet, dry or the lightly sparkling *perlé*) to a beautiful, sparkling *méthode gaillacoise ancestrale* that we tended to buy by the case and drink on the sun-drenched balcony.

This variety made for great tastings, as we were talked through the range of what the area had to offer and we always knew that there would be something for absolutely everyone to enjoy.

During our stay in Gaillac, we drank pretty much nothing apart from the local wines and were starting to really get a feel for how to select a good bottle and which names to look out for. I felt as if I was making great progress in unravelling some of my confusions about French wine. However, I was also acutely aware of what a small part of the French wine map Gaillac represented: if it took us two months to vaguely understand this small area, how would we ever get to grips with France as a whole?

★ ★ ★

After about three weeks in Gaillac, we flew back to the UK for the wedding of friends. It was a lovely service, and we had great fun catching up with old acquaintances, eating a ridiculous number of canapés and dancing very badly, but neither of us felt particularly that descending the steps from plane to Stansted runway was like coming home. After a few days, I was itching to get back.

By now it was early October, and the sun was still strong when we arrived back in Gaillac. The break had solidified our resolve to make a go of it in France and it was clear that this was no longer just a holiday: it was time to get serious and start putting down some roots. Money management was first on our list. We knew that we'd need a French bank account in order to get a lease on a flat in Lyon, so off we went to the bank.

We chose the bank that Jen had used when she'd lived in Paris, thinking that having records of at least one of us on the system might help navigate the warrens of bureaucracy and red tape that so many people had warned us about when we told them we were France-bound.

How wrong we were!

What followed was an immensely frustrating half-hour appointment that left us feeling pretty stressed and questioning whether we would be forced to return to the UK, defeated by the famous and inimitable French bureaucracy.

Could they find Jen on the system? Yes,

there was the account she'd had five years earlier. The strait-laced, dour-faced and grey-haired bank manager pointed to the entry on his computer screen.

Did this mean we could open an account with them? Not unless we had several proofs of our address in France.

Could we use the address that we would be staying at for another month? Not unless the utility bills were addressed to us. They weren't, of course: we were in a holiday let with all bills included in the rental.

Would this letter from Frankie, vouching that we were lodging with her, help at all? Not really: it wasn't a phone bill after all.

Hypothetically speaking, would we be able to sign a rental agreement in Lyon without having a current French bank account? Almost certainly not.

So, let me get this straight, to have a bank account in France you need an address in France, but to have an address in France you need to have a bank account? 'Yes, sir, that's correct.'

'Does that not seem like a rather flawed system to you?'

Blank expression.

'What would you suggest we do?'

'My advice would be to go back to the UK and find a job at a company who can send you out to France on business. Things tend to be easier for foreigners if they're set up with work.'

Unsurprisingly, the meeting finished pretty soon after that, and we both needed a calming beer at one of the cafés in the town square.

Thankfully, the following day we moved into L'Abeille and Frankie popped in to check how things were going. She snorted with laughter at our tale of woe with the spectacularly unhelpful bank manager, and offered to give someone a call at a different bank in the town. She had years of working as a private estate agent under her belt, and this gave her some clout. A couple of days later, passage smoothed in advance by a phone call to the bank manager, we had a much less stressful bank appointment, and came away with an account. Phew!

L'Abeille was a brilliantly pleasant surprise. The pictures we'd seen of the house online looked great — a big kitchen/dining room, with a little balcony overlooking the river that was just big enough for a table and chairs. There was a generous and comfortable master bedroom under the eaves, and a guest bedroom on the ground floor. What Frankie had decided to keep secret, though, was the upstairs sitting room. It was a gorgeous space with wooden beams in the ceiling and a huge amount of natural light from windows on three sides, including an enormous opening onto a stunning view out over the river. To the left, you could see the abbey and the bridge that led you across the river and into the town; to the right, the river curved away into the distance and the banks became more heavily wooded. One evening, we saw goats roaming in the undergrowth across the river from us, their bleating carrying across the water in the twilight.

★ ★ ★

One day, we woke up to the sound of rain hammering on the roof. It was the first drop of rain we'd had in over a month, and it actually felt very refreshing. Today would have to be an indoors day, and I decided to use it to get back on the cheese wagon. In all my exploring of the local area, I had been drawing frustrating blanks on the cheese front. Talking to market traders had led me to surmise that dairy farming around here was a rare and unprofitable thing. When I did eventually start work with Mons, and plotted the big cheeses on a map of France, I was interested to discover that, in picking Gaillac, we had in fact plumped for one of the most cheese-barren areas of the whole country to start our foodie French adventure. Whoops!

That said, there were a couple of interesting spots on the cheese tourist's road map not too far from us, although still a considerable drive away, notably, Rocamadour and Roquefort. I spent that rainy day planning exciting cheese excursions for us the following week.

Rocamadour is a stunning town in the Lot and well worth a visit, even if you aren't that into cheese. Nestled in a gorge among majestic, wooded valleys, the town is built vertically up a cliff face, its tall, bright white walls glinting in the midst of the surrounding green like something out of a Tolkien novel.

The cheese made in the area, and with which the town shares a name, is perhaps less majestic, a tiny disc of soft white goat's cheese — mild, with a lactic-acid tang and pleasing goat flavour that increases in intensity as the cheese ages and, in doing so, quickly dries out, concentrating the flavour. It's not a cheese that is going to fill you up, but it's a great little taste of the region, and a perfect addition to salads or simply eaten on the go.

My planned visit to Roquefort, on the other hand, was a bit of a fiasco. I had long been fascinated by the idea of visiting the famous caves in the commune of Roquefort-sur-Soulzon. These were formed in the collapse of the plateau of Combalou and are naturally cool, humid and very well ventilated. The story goes that a shepherd brought his fresh ewe's-milk curd here with a piece of bread. Then, distracted from his lunch (we presume by amorous intent), he left the cave. When he returned days later, the bread had gone mouldy and the blue mould had spread to the cheese.

There is an obvious question as to why the shepherd would then have tasted his mouldy cheese. My personal view on the matter is that humans have been around for long enough to try just about everything, and that this was really part of the natural food-selection process, evolving from the unlikely origins of some of our favoured foodstuffs into what we know today. Ultimately, if the cheese was really foul, we wouldn't be talking about it so many years later.

Well, it was a big drive away, but I was massively keen to visit. It was not until the morning of the departure, however, during one last Internet search to revise our itinerary, that I realized we had a problem. Due to the short lactation cycle of the ewe, the caves were filled with cheese only from January to June. For the rest of the year, plastic models are in place for the tourists. I was devastated, the trip was cancelled and I spent most of the rest of the day sulking on the balcony.

9

Lyonnais Living

Before we'd left London, I'd fired off an email to Hervé Mons on Jon Thrupp's instruction. Jon had primed Hervé first, explaining a bit about my situation and the fact that I was very keen to learn anything I could from him. Thus far, I'd received a fairly noncommittal response, but had noted that a certain Etienne Boissy had been cc'd in on the emails. I recognized his name from the signage of the shop in Lyon, and hoped that this meant I could get in on the action in Les Halles. The time for our move across the country to Lyon was approaching at speed, and I still had nothing close to a plan set up. I have to say, galvanizing myself to get organized at this stage had been a bit of a chore. The lazy, sunshine-filled days of complete freedom from responsibility could all too quickly get addictive. Jen was good at keeping me focused, though, even when she didn't mean to be. Occasionally, when she was working I'd hear the odd groan of frustration at a difficult email or a deadline with suddenly moveable goalposts emanating from the upstairs office (it was only fair that she claim the nicest room in the house to work from, after all).

I was getting good at providing freshly baked treats for her but I knew that all the madeleines in the world wouldn't make up for the fact that I might risk squandering the time off that I'd been given.

So I set to work. I sent chasers to Hervé and Etienne, letting them know my movements and stating again how enthusiastic I'd be to work for them. This time I emphasized pretty clearly that it was the experience, not the pay cheque, that I was after, and that basically I'd be happy to be a glorified tea boy and floor sweeper if it got me behind that hallowed cheese counter. I also started researching other Lyonnais *fromageries*, compiling a list of addresses that might be prepared to take me under their wings, even if only for a few weeks. To be honest, I was loath to get in touch with Hervé's competitors until I had had a more definite response from the man himself. The more research I did into Mons, the more I wanted to work there.

The organization had started with Hubert Mons, Hervé's father, when he began selling the excellent cheeses from his home region in the Auvergne at the markets around Roanne across the border in the Rhône-Alpes. Demand was strong and in the eighties the Mons name became firmly established through the opening of local shops and the network of maturing caves just outside the small village of Saint-Haon-le-Châtel.

Hervé was well known for his entrepreneurial spirit, and, since I'd seen him on a few YouTube videos, it wasn't hard to imagine him as the driving force for this expansion and investment. Laurent, his younger brother, took control of the retail side, while Hervé developed the *affinage* and export businesses. This was made possible through strong, carefully developed links with producers all over the country, allowing the organization to provide a well-rounded range.

The reputation of the company had grown, and in the early 2000s Hervé became one of the first of the Meilleurs Ouvriers de France (the best artisan craftsmen in France — often shortened to MOF) in the cheese category, securing his place among the French cheese elite. Laurent, for his part, masterminded the prestigious training school Opus Caseus Concept, which offered in-depth, expert training for French- and English-speaking cheese professionals.

During the decade that followed, Mons

had opened a number of new shops and expanded to the UK, Sweden and Japan, as well as forging strong links with the US — all the time with a focus on quality and connection to the producer. To match the expansion in volume of sales, the caves had been enlarged to include a nearby disused railway tunnel that had been converted into a stunning cheese-maturing cave.

Hervé and Laurent were outspoken and media-savvy; it wasn't hard to find them in interviews on the Internet and their passion and depth of understanding was clear to see. What appealed to me in particular was Hervé's business nous: he had succeeded in a significant vertical integration in the supply chain of artisanal/farmhouse cheese. By controlling both the *affinage* and retail, the company controlled a greater share not just of the margins, but also of the quality reaching the end user. This integration also pushed back up to the farmers, whom Hervé looked to be supporting by taking a fixed quantity of their output and also through feeding back his in-depth knowledge to help improve the *quality* of their output.

The combination of business acumen and a handle on the whole supply chain meant that Mons would clearly be a great place to learn a large amount about the trade. If they would take me on.

I hit send on my email, and hoped they would reply soon — the waiting was killing me!

* * *

Jen, meanwhile, was going great guns on the property-hunting front. She'd spent hours trawling the Internet for affordable flats in Lyon, and had drawn up a shortlist of possible rentals from a mixture of agents and private owners. We needed to find a furnished flat, which was a bit like gold dust, as the vast majority of leased properties in France are let completely bare. This, coupled with the fact that we were English, and therefore not in possession of a lot of the paperwork that was normally required by landlords and letting agencies, meant that several people weren't even prepared to let us come and view their properties.

'You could come and have a look around I suppose, but there's really not much point as your dossier will be far too weak for us to consider you.'

Ah, the dreaded dossier. In order to rent a flat in France, you have to submit a folder of paperwork to the landlord or the representative from the agency. This is a strict, detailed checklist of all the information you have ever possessed about all aspects of your life. They didn't require a list of every meal you'd ever eaten or a vial of your blood in order to secure the tenancy, but they weren't far off.

Our immediate problem was that several of these oh-so-important documents just didn't exist in the UK. There are rough equivalents, but they're not exactly the same. What's more, I was technically unemployed, and Jen had just signed onto the French freelancer scheme and had not yet got any tax documentation or indeed anything other than a couple of invoices to show for it. Nonetheless, we persevered, and I spent many, many hours (and toner cartridges) printing and photocopying any paperwork that could possibly be of use. Eventually, we hopped in the car with it all and drove the seven hours to Lyon to view some flats, hoping that, with our dossier as big as a dictionary and (ahem) charming personalities, someone would take pity on us and let us be their tenants.

★　★　★

It turned out that Lyon wouldn't be a city of strangers to us. By a lucky coincidence, a French friend of mine was living there. I had

125

first met Anne in London shortly after moving there for my role at the NAO. She was pretty and bright and rocked that classic, dark-haired, effortlessly sophisticated French look. She was living in east London and struggling to improve her English, despite working in an English-speaking environment, and I was looking to keep my French ticking over.

The classified-ads website Gumtree had brought us together and, over a year or so, we would meet regularly to try to teach each other our languages, but mostly we would go to exhibitions or, more likely, London pubs.

After she left London and continued her travels to Australia, we had both pretty much failed to stay in touch, with only the occasional email every few months. I was pretty sure, though, that either she was in Lyon or had been recently, so I sent an email asking if she was about and wanted to meet up while we were over there.

She replied immediately, saying that she was still in Lyon, that we should stay with her and she'd help us through the Lyon property rental assault course. I wasn't sure how she and Jen would get on, but I needn't have worried. That first evening we stayed up late in her small but cosy apartment, drinking copious glasses of red wine and discussing life, travel, the passage of time — and cheese.

It was great to know that, if we did ever find a flat in this city, we wouldn't be totally on our own.

* * *

As we started our search, we soon discovered that 'furnished' was a relative term. It seemed that, to class a flat as furnished in France, it has to contain a bed, a table, a fridge and a hotplate. Lots of the places we viewed were therefore minimal to say the least. We didn't have the funds to be able to invest in any furniture and, since wherever we ended up would be Jen's office as well as our home, we counted out a lot of places immediately due to their sparseness.

One place we visited was perfect. Light, airy and well maintained, with a separate bedroom and a well-equipped kitchen. It was in a nice area of town, up in the Croix-Rousse district on the hill, and it even had parking in a secure underground garage. On the phone with Jen, the landlady had seemed keen.

It should probably be mentioned here that Jen has a fantastic ear for accents, and, when she's having a good-French day, she really does sound French. She had obviously been having a good-French day on the phone to this potential landlady, whose face fell comically the moment she met us in person and realized we were English. It took some persuading for her to even take a look at our dossier, and, when barely a few hours later she called us to let us know our application had been unsuccessful, she decided to soften the blow by saying, 'Don't worry too much. We had a lovely Chinese couple come to look around yesterday. Their dossier was perfect but we didn't want to let it to them, either.' Good to know the xenophobia wasn't directed solely towards us Brits, then!

The next flat we saw, we really wanted. It was a studio, but a big one, on the fifth floor of an apartment block. It had wooden floors and high ceilings and had been lovingly, if slightly eccentrically, decorated and furnished by Audrey, a blonde twenty-something who had just purchased the flat when her boyfriend Seb asked her to move in with him. Audrey found our Englishness fascinating, despite not speaking a word of it herself. She could see we were both competent French speakers, and understood that communication wouldn't be an issue. Thankfully for us, she took us and our hotchpotch of a dossier seriously, working through our equivalent documentation slowly, and letting us explain our situation fully. As we left, she said there were several other couples in the frame, but that she'd be in touch soon.

'Soon' turned out to be the day after we'd arrived back in Gaillac. Audrey phoned Jen and gave her the good news: we'd got the flat! This meant getting back in the car for another cross-country drive to get contracts signed and paperwork sorted. Slightly alarmingly, she was already referring to us as '*mes petits Anglais*' when we arrived, and we were greeted with effusive hugs and kisses. She'd brought her boyfriend, her sister Céline and her brother-in-law Cyril along for the contract signing. There was much toasting with pastis, and we only felt *slightly* like animals in a zoo. 'Look, they're real live English people! And they're speaking *French*!'

I was hugely grateful to Audrey for taking a risk with our dossier, and it felt like a big weight off my mind to have a place to call home in Lyon for at least the next twelve months. We agreed a move-in date of 1 November, then went back west for our last week in Gaillac. We returned to the Château Bouscaillous, and bought a few cases of the sparkling wine we'd so loved, and generally made the most of our last few days in the autumn sunshine.

I had enjoyed small-town life. It was slow and easy and a wonderful change from hectic and polluted London. Of course, staying in a beautiful house with a guest room and choice of living rooms hadn't hurt, either. I was aware, though, that for me Gaillac had been a holiday and I couldn't afford to use my whole career break in that way. Lyon would be much more cramped and noisy (although nothing like as bad as London); it would be serious and the job hunting would begin in earnest.

And so, back in the car we went with our now much-travelled possessions! We were seasoned veterans of this drive by now, but each time we wove our way through the stunning scenery of the Gorges du Tarn, the fiery colours of the changing leaves never failed to take our breath away.

We spent that first night in Lyon at a hotel, so we could move in bright and early and jump through all the inventory sign-off hoops that we needed to with Audrey, before she'd hand over the keys.

We decided to go out to celebrate, and what better way than to visit a *bouchon*, one of Lyon's traditional eating establishments? The oft-repeated pop history was that the good cuts of meat went to Paris, and the secondary cuts went to Lyon. That was the reason why you had so many classic offal-based dishes in the region, and it was the *bouchons* that turned these classic dishes into generous and flavour-laden dining experiences.

Tripe, liver, chitterlings and pigs' feet were easy to find. I'm not going to lie, this wasn't for everyone, and, when I say everyone, I mean Jen.

She was game to try most things, but that first night we found an Achilles' heel in the form of a gelatinous *tête de veau*, a roulade of the slowly cooked flesh from inside a calf's head, bound up in copious quantities of rubbery fat. This was my chosen main course, and, as it came wobbling out to our table, I could see the colour drain from Jen's face. It was actually delicious, but she has nonetheless christened it 'the jelly sandcastle of evil'. It's a fair description, I must say. This wasn't a pretty or dainty dish. But, if you blindfolded me, I'd be happy to order it again and again. Also on the menu that night was *tablier de sapeur* — beaten and marinated tripe, deep-fried in breadcrumbs and served with a thick, creamy sauce a bit like a cross between mayonnaise and tartare. The restaurant was tiny, with tables pushed up against one another so that you couldn't help but get cosy with your fellow diners. The chef would wander out of the kitchen and sit and chat with his customers at the small, square, wooden tables that were decked out in red-and-white-chequered cloth. He took the time to explain to us the history of the dishes. It was a brilliant and unusual approach to running a restaurant.

We soon found that we were chatting to the adjacent couple, sharing our food and discussing what the Lyonnais culinary scene had to offer. It was a perfect introduction to the city, and we decided that we were probably going to like it here!

10

Festive *Fromage*

I'd been enjoying exploring Lyon, finding new local shops and points of interest. Anne had trained as a tour guide, and was brilliant at helping us find quirky corners and teaching us about the history of some of the tourist attractions. Even with a wealth of new things to discover, I did still find myself lurking around the cheese counters of Les Halles on a fairly regular basis. I introduced myself to Etienne on one of these occasions, but received a fairly harassed look of not-quite-recognition, and I ended up buying an enormous quantity of a ruinously expensive triple-creamed cheese with a vein of truffle running through it to cover my embarrassment.

Then, a couple of weeks later, I had a reply from one of my many emails to Etienne and Hervé. Hervé would be visiting the Lyon shop the following week, and would I like to come in for a quick chat?

Yes, yes, I would, thank you very much!

So finally this was it; my first meeting with

Hervé Mons, the head honcho, the big cheese, the man to impress. I had done my homework, studying some of the many interviews with him that had been posted on YouTube, so I knew more or less what to expect: a blisteringly fast delivery, strewn with slang, obscure idioms and wrapped up neatly in a rich and, to my ear at least, largely impenetrable Auvergnat accent.

I didn't like my chances.

I nervously made my way to the shop. Autumn was petering out into the icy clutches of winter; it was cold and crisp and I was feeling alive. Les Halles were at a low ebb, normal for a weekday afternoon. I was a little early, so I took a slow tour of the now familiar sights, bright lights and beautifully presented produce. Was this now nearer to my grasp? I bloody hoped so!

I met Etienne in the shop. His big welcoming smile put me at ease as my hand was shaken before I was ushered upstairs. The first floor of the shop in Les Halles houses a small office, but the space is mainly taken up by a small restaurant, where shoppers can take a break, sit down and relax with a plate of cheeses and a glass of wine, or, in the winter months, a bubbling pot of gooey fondue while they reflect on the day's purchases. The space is warm, dark and intimate, with a hanging along one wall which depicts the Tunnel de la Collonge, Hervé's much-prized cheese-ageing cave converted from a section of an abandoned railway tunnel.

Hervé's presence in this environment transforms it completely. This comfortable area becomes a place of business, where tough negotiations are held and brave new plans are hatched and put into motion. As I came up from the shop, he was sitting in the office in a crisp white shirt, leaning back with his arms behind his head; he could have been the diagram in a book showing dominance through body language.

After a very quick introduction from Etienne and a firm shake of the hand, Hervé got straight to the point.

'So, Matt, you want to work for me for free?'

'No,' I stumbled, the French words feeling suddenly more foreign than ever, 'I want to work for you for the experience.'

He looked at me and smiled slowly, not saying anything. The silence probably lasted only a few seconds but to me it felt like hours. Suddenly, he sat up straight, rubbed his hands together and said, 'OK, Etienne will be in touch later this month.'

And, with that, the meeting was over. It

had lasted all of forty-five seconds, but there was certainly a glimmer of hope. I felt just that one small step closer to getting my hands on the cheese.

★ ★ ★

I didn't hear anything again for a week. Then another week rolled by, and another, and before long I was getting quite panicky. I was keen to work. I would have started the very next day, or even that afternoon if they'd let me. At the same time, though, I didn't want to appear too needy. As Lyon got progressively colder and Christmas trundled towards us like a tinsel-wrapped juggernaut, I was beginning to lose hope in Hervé and Etienne, and I was in the process of rewriting my CV and covering letter (again) and dusting off my list of other cheese shops in the area to bombard with the hope of some experience over the festive period, even if it was just handling the broom and cleaning the windows. It had been three months since we had moved to France and I still had no real work experience to show for it.

I persevered with Mons, as my research had, if anything, heightened my desire to work there. The organization was far-reaching and ticked so many of the boxes for what I was trying to achieve. I wasn't sure that working in an independent cheese shop would give me the access to wholesale and *affinage*, or critically to the producers who had been, up to this point, pretty dismissive of my efforts to get in contact.

So I continued to chase, about once a week, until suddenly there was a breakthrough. Etienne rang me and asked for a copy of my CV and told me that I needed to attend the team meeting where the Christmas period would be discussed and I would be given my timetable for a two-week internship!

★   ★   ★

The weekend before the meeting, Jen and I decided to drive from Lyon to Florence to visit my parents. We had been saying that we would visit for over a month, and now it looked like my free time might become a bit more limited. Also, it now seemed highly unlikely that we would be able to visit them over Christmas.

We set off, placing a frankly stupid amount of trust in our satnav, which we had named Daniel. He had confidently informed us that the journey through the Alps would take around seven hours. Daniel, it turns out, is a liar. As we entered our eleventh hour on the road, it was dark and we were navigating steep, winding and unkempt roads on the outskirts of Florence. The gnarled olive trees looked imposing as their craggy trunks caught the beams of the headlights through the hammering rain, and both Jen and I were seriously starting to question whether the trip was worth the effort!

We needn't have worried: no sooner had we arrived at my parents' holiday rental in Fiesole and cracked open the first bottle of Prosecco than the long and painful journey was forgotten.

My parents were in Italy at the start of what they were terming an 'old person's gap year' — soaking up the art, the language and, of course, the food. In the space of two days, we packed away mounds of butter-yellow, fresh pasta, wild-boar ragout, garlicky brus-chetta and creamy tiramisu. It was great to see my parents, and it took my mind off my nerves for the upcoming meeting in Lyon.

★ ★ ★

When it did come time to meet the team I hoped would become my future colleagues, I was too excited to be nervous.

I arrived at Les Halles to find that the Christmas decorations had gone up, the *ambiance* was more spectacular than ever, the numerous oyster bars were buzzing and the atmosphere was raucous.

The upstairs restaurant at the shop was filling up and there were a lot of new faces, all of whom knew each other and were eager to catch up. It also seemed that they had all heard of the Englishman who was coming to try his hand at cheesemongering.

I had my name-learning hat on and was doing my best to try to remember the key names while my French floundered a little in the face of the very argumentative style of discussion.

There was Séverine, who appeared to be Etienne's right-hand woman in the shop. She was moon-faced and smiley, with glasses and short, neat hair. Lounging against a wall near the back of the room was Guillaume, who looked to be about my age, with thick eyebrows and an intense look on his face. Gossiping and laughing across the table in the corner were two girls named Lola and Eloïse. They were working at the shop while they trained for a commercial diploma, and were occasionally reprimanded for not taking the cheese as seriously as they could have. Justine was there, too. Even without being introduced to her I could tell she was Etienne's daughter — the family resemblance was striking. Last to arrive before Hervé and Etienne started the meeting was Sabrina, a slender woman with Tunisian heritage, who came pelting up the stairs and sat down just in time, a flustered frown on her face.

I did my best to follow the rapid-fire French and cheese-specific vocabulary as I flicked through my pile of documents, eventually finding the important one: my schedule. I was a little shocked to discover that a huge number of hours had been allotted to me, and that I would be allowed only two days off — Christmas Day and New Year's Day. I had never worked around Christmas like that before, and, to be honest, had never spared a thought for those who did. I quickly added a few good books to my shopping list for Jen — all of our friends would be leaving Lyon to spend Christmas with family, so it was going to be a fairly solitary one for her while I toiled away at the cheesy coalface.

As the meeting progressed, I was asked, individually, by just about everyone on the team, 'So, what exactly are you doing here?' The general consensus among the staff was that, if you could work as a reasonably well-paid accountant, why on earth would you want to come and work in an industry that tends not to pay much above the minimum wage? It was a good question, but by then I had been asked so many times that my answer was getting better.

★　★　★

On my first day of work experience I arrived at the shop on time, halfway between bleary and ecstatic. Etienne and Guillaume had already been there for an hour, unloading the large delivery of cheese, and they were now in the shop, busily preparing the display. There were trays of cheese everywhere, covering all surfaces, as their contents were carefully distributed to fill the holes left by cheese-hungry clients the evening before.

I headed upstairs to grab my uniform — a Mons-branded T-shirt with 'Staff' written on the back — and a brown Mons-branded apron — and then headed down to the shop to help. I was tasked with primping and preening the cheeses, lining them up and rotating the stock, cutting off the tired-looking bits and generally making the shop look as sexy as possible. It was explained to me that, for any cheese not sold whole, an example would always be cut, as it was significantly less intimidating for the customer. Understandable really: we all know how attractive a cleanly cut cheese can be, showing off at once its rind and hidden interior. With this in mind, Guillaume asked me to cut a couple of the Brillat Savarin in two with a lyre — essentially a metal hoop with a cheese wire stretched between the two arms. I think he assumed that I had done this before — I hadn't, of course. Completely ignorant of correct technique, I made a fair stab at it, and was pleased with the result. Then, taking two of the cut pieces in hand, I leaned over the display to neatly place them ready for sale. As I did this, my elbow knocked one of the remaining pieces to the floor, where it landed wetly, cut face down.

A quick glance around seemed to suggest that no one had seen my 'accident', but I couldn't be sure. I instinctively picked up the cheese and cut off the bit that had come into contact with the floor. Should I confess? Should I let them know of my failing less than five minutes in? What if they'd seen me and I said nothing? I would be dishonest in their eyes. I couldn't cope with this level of stress!

In the end I confessed. No one seemed to care. The cheese was fine. The bit that I had cut off was probably only a five-centime loss to them, and, considering that we were entering the two biggest sales weeks of the year, it just didn't matter. Phew!

* * *

It was clear from the outset that I would not be serving customers. First, my French wasn't good enough; second, I had no relevant experience; third, and perhaps most important, my understanding of the range of cheeses was just too limited. Having seen the chaos that the servers were dealing with, the sea of Christmas shoppers waiting for service (some not too patiently), I was perfectly happy with this arrangement. I hoped that I would get there one day, but for now I was content to be *en bas* — below stairs — working peacefully with the cheeses.

Just as the shop had an upstairs, a cosy restaurant ideal for whiling away the hours while nibbling on fine cheese and quaffing good wine, it also had a downstairs, called the *labo*. This area included a large walk-in fridge, a wonderfully dark, cool and humid cave for storing all of the cheese, and a fair amount of workspace on which one could perform all manner of cheese prep.

The *labo* had a door out to the basement level of Les Halles, which is completely unseen by the general public. It has exactly the same layout as the glitzy ground floor but none of the decoration. The bare concrete is grubby-looking and its use is purely functional. To me it was a wonderful contrast to the perfection of the shops, which can all become a little draining after a while, particularly at Christmas time when you can barely move for visitors.

The long corridors sport sturdy overhead rails that the butchers use to transport heavy carcasses hanging on hooks with wheels, like inverted pointy roller skates. During the day, these rails would rattle with the passing caravans of top-quality meat. You needed to stop, look and listen before leaving the safety of the *labo*: the consequences of being hit by a menagerie of carcasses travelling at top speed didn't bear thinking about.

The underground of Les Halles was where the magic happened, the staging ground for what was to be sold above. Looking through those doors (on the rare occasions that they were open) was to peek through a window into all manner of specialist industries, from butchery to fishmongery, cold-smoking to oyster shucking. It was a hive of activity, and also where the traders would come for a cigarette break and the chance to have five minutes away from the relentless madness of their respective shops during the Christmas rush.

*   *   *

My tasks were relatively straightforward, but I was very pleased with how hands-on they were. Mainly I was working with Guillaume, preparing orders for the restaurants that the shop supplies. Initially, restaurants would have placed orders with Hervé and the Mons caves in Saint-Haon, but, since their growth spurt, dealing with restaurants had been delegated, appropriately in my opinion, to the Mons shops. Lyon is well placed in that, using a national refrigerated-transport company, we were able to make next-day deliveries to pretty much anywhere in France, even during the busy Christmas week.

We would track down the required cheeses in line with the order and the specifications that it contained, such as maturity, weight and any degree of pre-cutting. Then we would wrap them up, box them up and ship them out. This exercise showed me immediately how much I still had to learn. Just recognizing the cheeses was hard enough to start with. On top of that, knowing what level of maturity would be appropriate for a restaurant was far from straightforward. Finally, how do you wrap a cheese? I was shown, of course, but it was surprisingly fiddly, and maintaining both standards and speed was critical.

On top of this work there was the full-time

requirement to make sure that the shop was appropriately stocked. With the high volume of sales came a scarily quick rate of shelf depletion. Lists of cheeses to fill the gaps would arrive downstairs via the cramped lift at regular intervals. I would do my best to hunt out the requested cheeses and send them up to the shop. Again, not mind-blowing work, but I was quickly learning to recognize more and more cheeses by sight.

Hervé was fairly often present during this time, working on the preorders that customers had made to avoid the queues during the Christmas week. Watching him work was like watching a machine: controlled, efficient and inhumanly fast. He was breaking down cheeses at lightning speed, working on several orders at once, never getting lost, never slowing down. I was awestruck. It was amazing to see a boss back on the floor and so skilled at his work.

He gave me things to do, not because he needed to, but because he wanted me to have the experience. I handled myself OK, but really it takes experience to cut cheese well, and, even with advice from one of the best, I was making all kinds of mistakes. Thankfully, the industry is relatively forgiving of poorly cut bits of cheese: if they aren't absolutely perfect, most customers really don't mind (within reason), and, in fact, making it look machine-cut is something to avoid!

If you've really made a mess of a cut, you can always cut out a few neat slices for restaurant clients, and the rest can be cut up into cubes for people to try while they're queuing.

★ ★ ★

Christmas with Jen was a snatched affair, a day and a half's respite in the middle of a storm of long, physically demanding hours (for an overweight accountant at least), and foreign-language-induced headaches.

Hervé presented me with a huge box of cheese for us, to thank me for the work that I had put in, well over 2 kilos in total, which we chomped through enthusiastically!

The time flew by and before long I was finishing up for New Year's Eve, exhausted, having worked from 7 a.m. to 8 p.m. with a brief pause for lunch, but elated nonetheless.

As I was preparing to stagger home and hoping that I would be able to keep my eyes open long enough to see in the New Year, Hervé told me that, if I was keen to pursue further experience with him and the company, he would be glad to discuss it with me, and he'd be in touch once things had calmed down a bit.

★ ★ ★

This time I didn't have to wait long. In a couple of weeks, I was summoned back to the office above the shop, where Hervé and Etienne were waiting for me, their expressions unreadable.

'Matt, we liked the way that you handled yourself and we want to offer you a job,' Hervé started, 'but first you need to learn the trade; you need to spend time in the caves.'

This was amazing, better than I could have hoped for. He wanted me to spend two to three months in the caves before taking on a position in the shop in charge of stock and restaurant orders.

There were conditions, though.

'We will take you on as paid employee if we are happy with your progress. While you're training in the caves, I won't be able to pay you, but I can provide accommodation.'

OK, I thought, I can cope with that. I could feel a pretty huge grin forming on my face.

'One more thing, Matt,' Hervé added nonchalantly. 'For this to work for us, we need you to be able to speak French like a Frenchman.'

My smile froze slightly on my face. These were some pretty big conditions to meet. I think the word I was looking for was *merde*!

★ ★ ★

I am not particularly gifted with languages.

This admission surprises people when I talk to them, particularly in French. I am now fluent but I know enough about the language-learning process to know that I will never be truly bilingual, nor will I lose my English accent — not that I would really want to.

Learning French has been a pleasure for me, and if it hadn't been I certainly wouldn't have carried on doing it, but it has taken a huge amount of time and effort, probably not far off what I put into my chemistry degree.

My father is a fluent French speaker and my mother's French is good. They had spent a fair amount of time out there after all, and were much more immersed than it's possible to be now with the ubiquity of the Internet and Anglophone press. The reason I managed to scrape a 'B' in my French GCSE was largely due to serious coaching from my, seemingly frustrated, parents, my father in particular not appearing to understand the difficulty I had in putting together phrases and learning grammar and words.

Looking back on it now, I don't blame him. It wasn't until I took up French in an evening class in preparation for moving to Aix that I realized quite how incorrectly I had approached the process of language learning at school. I had previously believed that it was necessary to say a sentence, reciting it from memory as it were, rather than forming it from the relevant nouns and verbs. This was a revelation, and within weeks I had long surpassed the level that I had acquired at school. I was enjoying hitting the books and, for the first time in a non-sciency subject, I was enjoying the process.

Of course my time in Aix taught me a huge amount of French and I returned confident, but far from perfect. I could make myself understood and mostly I could understand what people were saying to me, but I lacked the depth and familiarity with a wider vocabulary, which made my conversations a little stilted. In addition, I had picked up a bad habit of overthinking my word choice to ensure that I wasn't making mistakes, meaning I spoke veeerrrrry sloowwwly.

In fact, that kind of self-correction marks you out as someone not particularly at ease. You're far better off in 99 per cent of cases just getting the words out and accepting that it won't be perfect. Most native French speakers will be grateful for your efforts, and happy to help you out. Certainly there will be some that are difficult, but are those really the kinds of people that you want to be friends with? There are those occasions, though, where your mistakes leave you no other option than to accept some mockery.

A particularly humiliating case in point was a shopping experience pretty soon after we moved to France. I was at the market, looking for ingredients to prepare a traditional roast dinner with all the trimmings, and thought that I might try duck-fat roast potatoes, rather than the more common goose-fat variety — it couldn't hurt to be adventurous, after all.

Having spied a butcher with what looked like the very duck fat that I required, I queued up politely before saying in my very best French, 'Bonjour, je me demandais si vous avez la graisse du connard?'

This was met with a Gallic snort of derision, which was not surprising since I had very politely asked him if he had any 'bastard grease' — the word that I had been looking for was of course canard. I'm not sure what 'bastard grease' might be, but I reckon it wouldn't have proven to be the best cooking medium for roasties!

★ ★ ★

Hervé was giving me a month to learn to speak French like a Frenchman — I had some serious work to do!

11

The Training Begins

My first day of training at the caves was to be Monday, 27 February 2012. I was down for a 7 a.m. start and so had taken the tactical decision to get there the night before, making sure that I was nice and rested for my first day at school. I had put a lot of effort into getting here and the thought of having to be civil to new people in a foreign language after having got up at four in the morning and driven for two hours didn't feel like the best way to get started. Mons owned a property known simply as 'the Villa', and I would be staying here during the week over the next few months, a stone's throw from all the cheese-ageing cave action.

The journey to Saint-Haon that night was uneventful. I knew the way already and the traffic on a Sunday evening was calm. Small flurries of snowflakes were occasionally lit up in the beams of my headlights, and my stomach was knotted in excitement. I was like a kid on Christmas Eve, and I couldn't wait to finally have the chance to get some real cheese experience. There would surely be lots of early mornings and some very hard work, but getting my hands dirty in this industry that had captivated my attention really appealed, particularly after the last six months of unemployed wandering. Don't get me wrong, I had loved the freedom of the last five or six months — the lie-ins, the exploring, and the opportunity to spend lots of time with Jen — but the whole reason I was in France was to get as much hands-on experience in cheese as I possibly could. As I drove past the cave complex on my way to the Villa, locked and in darkness for the night, I sincerely hoped that it wouldn't be a case of the grass always being greener.

Now, when I talk about ageing caves, or just 'the caves', I ought to make it clear that I'm not really talking about underground rocky grottos but rather, manmade environments in which cheeses can be aged. Perhaps 'cellar' is a better translation, although, of course, historically, the ageing process would most likely have been undertaken in genuine caves, as a cool temperature and high humidity are great for storing and improving cheeses. In some cases, genuine caves are still used such as in Roquefort, but mostly we have opted for a more controllable, artificially created environment. That's not to say, however, that manmade caves can't be dank and atmospheric. I have vivid memories of visiting our producer of Saint-Nectaire, a flattish disc weighing in at around 1.5 kilos with a grey rind, a mellow, yellow fruity pâte. The rind tastes and smells like the cave, dripping wet and pungent with damp straw underfoot. You didn't want to be leaning against those walls.

★ ★ ★

I arrived at the car park of the Villa a little later than expected, having got lost because the satnav didn't recognize the street that the place was on. I had driven in circles through the small village, which boasted not much more than a pretty church and a post office, until a local man had taken pity on me and my evident lost state and pointed out the small side road that I had somehow not seen.

After ringing Jen to let her know that I had survived the journey and wasn't upside down in a ditch, I knocked on the door and was greeted by Aurélie, the Mons communications officer. The warm light escaping from the living room windows bathed the large garden in gold. Despite the chill in the air, I was content to hang back a moment before entering. It was a long time since I had been anywhere this silent at night.

Aurélie was also living in the Villa on a temporary basis while renovations were being made to the local flat that she had recently purchased. She was deeply immersed in the Mons family and had previously lived in Lyon, working in the Mons shop there with Etienne. She opened the door with a smile and welcomed me inside. She had dark hair and a smattering of freckles across her nose. She also looked completely exhausted and was wearing pyjamas. I checked my watch — 9 p.m.

Aurélie gave me a quick tour of the Villa, yawning expansively as she did so. It was large and open but sparsely furnished. There wasn't much to do except eat, sleep and work, but that was fine: from what I could imagine, everyone passing through, whether they were interns or international tradesmen, knew exactly why they were there and generally didn't need to do much more than eat, sleep and work.

'Here's the kitchen,' she said, pointing. 'It's a pretty informal set-up. Generally, everyone just chips in for the food and whoever feels like being the chef can make enough for everyone. I'm sorry but I have to get some sleep now, and you should, too — big day tomorrow.'

I nodded and bade her goodnight, content to poke about in the kitchen for a few minutes before bed. Aurélie turned on her way upstairs. 'Oh, I forgot to say: on the subject of cooking . . . '

'Yes?'

'I'm allergic to gluten. And . . . er . . . lactose.' She smiled sheepishly as my face fell and I felt my repertoire of recipes shrink by about two-thirds. 'Sorry, chef. *Bonne nuit.*'

Even before I'd seen her at work, I was already massively impressed by her dedication in continuing to work in such a lactose-heavy environment. She later explained that she was such a huge fan of cheese that it was worth the pain sometimes. It also elevated cheese to a real luxury, a treat item for her, meaning that she would occasionally select a few of the very best cheeses that the caves had to offer, and would never take the quality for granted.

I headed quickly up to my new bedroom, not large, but by no means tiny, with a double bed, a small rickety desk, a chair and a cupboard. The bed was comfortable and I was tired, but sleep was hard to come by. The pressure to perform, trowelled on generously by Hervé in our earlier meeting, was weighing heavily on my mind. When playing the 'what's the worst that could happen?' game, I've proved myself to have a pretty fertile imagination.

★ ★ ★

I woke at six, showered, shaved and mentally prepared myself to try to be on top form. It was dark outside, and icy cold. Black coffee was drunk, so strong it was almost sticky. It was clear that the recent few months of unemployment had ill-prepared me for being awake this early — I should have tried to get some practice in.

I shared a ride into the caves with Aurélie. It was five minutes' walk away at most but we were running late and she decided it would be easiest to drive. There had been a heavy frost overnight but we were running too late to scrape the windscreen. 'Trust me,' said Aurélie, speeding out of the Villa's driveway, 'you do not want to be late for Hervé on your first day. He hates tardiness.' She was giving me a meaningful look as she spoke, but I wished she'd focus more on the road! The gap in the iced-up window through which we observed the outside world was tiny. It was fortunate that there was little traffic, because I doubt we would have seen it and our road positioning was anybody's guess.

We arrived in the large car park in one piece, as much, I believe, through luck as driving skill. The sun was slowly rising over the frosted, misty fields, deep red and ripe with opportunity.

The car park was already a hive of activity as the *affineurs* arrived. The Mons organization has seen significant growth in recent years and to make best use of the space and diverse shipping hours, there were two dispatch shifts, the first starting at 4 a.m. or 5 a.m., the second at 1 p.m. and running through until 8 p.m. Overlapping these two shifts were the *affineurs*: they started at 7 a.m. and worked through until 4 p.m. I would be following their timetable.

Aurélie whisked me hastily to the locker area, which was in the material storage part of the caves, a big, shedlike structure where one is surrounded by looming towers of cheese paraphernalia, neatly organized in rows and shelves, from cardboard boxes to cheese wires, bags of dried ceps to branded T-shirts.

I was introduced to numerous new faces (their names disconcertingly falling out of my head almost as soon as they were mentioned) and I was presented with my cheese uniform, consisting of a branded white fleece, a branded brown overcoat and a branded brown apron. I was wearing steel-toe-capped, white cheese clogs and a hairnet, and I must say I was looking quite the part.

I made my way into the main preparation area with the rest of the *affineurs*. There, the *fromagères* were hard at work, nipping from cave to cave, selecting cheeses, cutting, wrapping, boxing up and shouting. There were more hellos and more names to try to remember. I suddenly realized that I was doing it all wrong: everyone was doing the kissing thing to say hello, but I had been shaking hands. Did that set me apart immediately as an unknowledgeable outsider, an uptight foreigner lacking even the most primitive of social skills? Do you *faire la bise* (do the kiss) on a first meeting or not? And is there ever an appropriate moment to ask that question?

Toiling with this conundrum, I failed to notice that the rest of the *affineurs* had vanished. I couldn't find them anywhere. I went hunting for them, changing shoes (there were inside-shoe/outside-shoe rules in place here) so that I could go outside to see if they were on a smoking break, changing back to see if they were in the offices, checking all of the individual caves to see if they were handling the cheeses.

I finally found them in the middle of the morning team briefing with Hervé. I scuttled in at the back, and noticed Hervé's eyebrows knit together slightly as he spotted me. Late. Damn!

He was already in full flow, sitting at the head of the table wearing his Mons baseball cap. The sleeves of his work coat were rolled up and ready for business. He was talking about his recent international cheese diplomacy visit to Australia. 'We need to up our game,' he said, in his rapid-fire, staccato French. 'The cheese wrapping that they're doing over there is so precise it's scientific.' He paused, and gestured to a stool near the front of the room. 'Everyone, this is Matt, from England. He's here to learn the ropes so he can work in the Lyon shop. Show him everything he needs to know. Do not go easy on him.' He softened this rather brusque introduction by handing me a small wooden keyring in the shape of a boomerang, before launching back into his report on Australia's cheesemongers without missing a beat.

The morning briefings were held in the small reception to the complex. This was where the coffee machine was and it therefore served as the social centre of the caves. The briefings covered what the *affineurs* intended to achieve that day and who would be doing it. Any issues in terms of quality would be discussed and wrinkles in the general running of the caves would be firmly flattened by Hervé in his classic forceful style. The old adage that one should not bring problems to one's boss, but rather offer solutions, did not necessarily ring true here. Hervé loved to solve problems. A brief discussion of the relative merits of each potential course of action would be undertaken before a swift ruling was made and that was that — bring on the next item of business. Coming from an industry that often spends a long time in meetings worrying out issues, I found that this decision-making speed was refreshing.

It was decided that for the first couple of weeks I would work with the *affineurs* to get a good handle on the cheeses, where they could be found and how to recognize the different levels of *affinage* in each one. Then I would be rotated to work with the *fromagères*, learning about order preparation. I would also spend some time with Alain, a jovial former teacher who worked across the two teams, charged with opening the big cheeses for the *fromagères* and dispatching prepared palettes to their national or international destinations. He had a date with a wheel of Parmesan that needed to be opened later that day and suggested to Hervé that I join in to see how it was done.

For the morning, my task was to help the

affineurs work the drying room, or *hâloir*.

An *hâloir* is essentially a relatively cool and slightly humid environment that allows the cheese to reduce its humidity slowly through evaporation. Without this step, when the cheese enters the cave and warms up slightly, the bacteria and moulds in and on the rind accelerate their action rapidly in the lovely wet environment of the cheese and, before you know it, just below the rind, the cheese turns very liquid. This results in what is known as 'toad's skin', whereby the cheese becomes very difficult to handle. When you pick it up, the cheese will stay there but the skin will come away in your fingers.

Deciding whether a cheese is ready to leave the *hâloir* is a question of feeling the cheese to judge its dampness and considering its physical appearance. Almost as soon as I arrived, I was told in a tone that brooked no argument that it takes nine months to get on top of the process. The problem with farm-produced cheeses is that they are variable, they have different moisture con-tents, they may be of slightly different shapes and they may have received a different amount of salt. On top of that, the position of the cheese in the crate will determine how quickly it loses humidity.

Essentially, even cheeses made on the same

day by the same farmer with the same milk will mature differently, so the *affineur* has to treat each one individually and stream them accordingly.

In practical terms, you take a tall trolley containing a stack of crates full of cheeses from the *hâloir*. You take one crate at a time and you take each cheese within that crate and transfer it, while turning it, to a new, empty crate, separating out all those that are ready for the cave into a separate crate. The cheeses requiring more '*hâloir* love' go back and get it, and those that are ready to take the next leap and grow some real character move on to the cave.

Turning a cheese is massively important. You want this thing to grow up to be as homogeneous as possible, after all, so you need to ensure that all of the rind is exposed to the same conditions. The face of a cheese that is against a flat surface has no oxygen, while the other side is in the atmosphere. It's only natural that under these conditions the two sides will develop differently. At the *hâloir* stage, it's particularly important to make sure that the cheese doesn't stay on one surface for too long, since this obviously will affect the rate at which humidity leaves the cheese.

Patting down cheese is important, too. The

moulds growing on the cheeses need to be controlled to ensure that they don't get out of hand, and also that they help in the formation of a healthy rind. Left to their own devices, cheeses often end up looking like furry little kittens.

It wouldn't be wrong to say that all you have to do is rub and turn the cheese, then put it in a new crate, but the subtle differences in humidity that you are required to spot make the process quite involved. During that first week, I would ask the other *affineurs* for an example of a cheese that was good to age, and one that should stay in the *hâloir*, and I would keep them apart to use as references.

I had never had the opportunity to touch so much cheese in my life! On my first morning, we were dealing with the new arrivals from the Touraine from the end of the week before. This area of France is renowned for its goat's cheeses, particularly the Sainte-Maure de Touraine, the Valençay, the Selles-sur-Cher and the Pouligny-Saint-Pierre. Of these, it was the Sainte-Maure that I knew best. A log-shaped cheese with a straw running through the middle, it had a rind that was blackened by vegetable cinders and had a great goaty taste with a lick of animal and stable and just enough acidity to stop the centre from cloying. As it is aged, the brittle, friable centre turns creamy and the potency can go through the roof, depending on how it's matured of course. It was a mild form of torture to be around so much delicious cheese and not be able to taste it, and I got used to the sound of my stomach rumbling pretty much constantly.

I was mid-cheese-flipping when Alain came to find me to let me know that he was ready to open the Parmesan. The fact that such a big deal had been made out of it implied that this would be a pretty serious event. I was more than happy to put down my Valençay and follow him.

There was a kind of ritual to his process which I admired. He took his time, carefully selecting his tools and double-checking their cleanliness. He would make sure that he had sufficient space and that all was prepared before even touching the cheese. He had a Zen approach that was far removed from the blurring hands of the *affineurs*. 'It's a hard cheese to open, if you rush it, you'll cut it badly and probably hurt yourself,' he said, as he sized up his cheesy opponent.

I knew a fair bit about Parmesan, or Parmigiano-Reggiano, as the Italians call it, as I had been reading up on my cheeses and watching YouTube videos on how to open them. I knew that traditionally a wheel of Parmesan would be opened with a set of specialist knives with flat, 10-centimetre-long blades. These would be inserted and wiggled to find and exploit the natural weaknesses in the wheel, splitting the cheese and leaving a wonderfully pungent but very uneven surface, giving a great idea of how the curds hold together to form the finished cheese. This opening method is considered to respect the texture of the cheese.

Alain explained to me that in the Mons caves, however, it is done differently. We use a very long, extra-thick cheese wire to cut the cheese neatly in half, the benefit being a much lower surface area to lose humidity and flavour, with the advantage that it is easier to wrap closely once cut to further reduce undesired loss of water.

Following a thorough rubbing to buff up the rind, remove any undesired mould, and reduce the oiliness of the cheese (it can be mighty slippery to try to get a handle on) the cheese would be lifted onto a trolley — no mean feat given that most Parmesans weigh around 40 kilos. An incision is made around the circumference with a strange-looking hooked knife that has a blade that curves to a point perpendicular to the handle. It's designed to cut only a few millimetres deep, just enough to get through the thick rind. This in itself is hard work, as the pressure required to cut leaves you with a tendency to deviate from the central line. Once all the way around, a second cut is made along the same line, but at an angle, so as to remove a small wedge of rind from the circumference of the cheese.

Then, with the cheese against your chest (to stop it falling onto the floor) you take a double-handled knife and cut towards yourself through the nick in the rind to a depth of a few centimetres. This gives the cheese wire a much-needed helping hand.

Then for the difficult bit. The thick cheese wire is looped around the cheese, slotting neatly into the nick you've just made. You hold the wire next to the cheese with your left hand, while putting your left knee against the cheese and then leaning back almost horizontally so that your weight is applied to the cheese wire through your right hand, which you lock into your right side. The wire doesn't budge until you turn your whole upper body, forcing the wire through the cheese.

This method is almost like a form of cheese ballet — it requires strength and technique. Unfortunately, I was not able to demonstrate either and really made little impact on the cheese. Alain, the prima ballerina, took over, and sliced through the enormous cheese with impressive fluidity.

As I went back to turning the goat's cheeses, I realized just how much I had to learn.

12

On *Affinage*

The role of the *affineur* is rather complex, but at its root it is simply the process of making a given cheese as 'fine' as it can be.

Now, before I start this chapter, I ought to say that I know that technically speaking '*affineur*' isn't an English word, but for me 'cheese maturer' or some other similar title just doesn't really cut it.

It's a funny thing learning completely new vocab in a foreign language: often, you never get around to learning the English equivalent of a word, especially if it has limited use and you only ever talk about it to people who don't communicate with you in English.

What I'm trying to say is that I would never describe the job that I was doing as cheese maturing. It was *affinage*, and I was working with a team of *affineurs*. It doesn't require translation, although, of course, some explanation wouldn't be a bad idea.

There are other English translations that don't sit right with me. For example, I can't get on at all with the use of 'paste' (meaning the middle of the cheese) instead of the French *pâte*. It just isn't right.

Anyhoo, back to the caves . . .

★ ★ ★

Over the course of my first month or so at the caves with the *affineurs*, my goal was to learn not just the names and characteristics of the cheeses in the Mons range (around two hundred in number) but also how the company went about ageing them. This understanding is pretty critical for someone working in the business, as cheese really is a developing thing: over time it will change in taste, texture and appearance. With a greater experience of how and why cheese ages in the way it does, you can control its development, improving it, or at least preventing it from deteriorating, and you can recognize problems more quickly, often simply by eye or nose.

Sometimes cheese feels almost alive in the way it develops, and in fact that's not too far from the truth. The chemical and biological processes going on in that little lump of curd are really rather complex and, to me at least, completely fascinating.

Affinage is about controlling the digestion of the young cheese with enzymes. Enzymes

171

are nature's little helpers; they are created and used by living organisms to interact with (and usually digest) the world around them.

The enzymes that we're talking about here come from the milk itself, the rennet that we added to make the cheese and, most importantly, from the microbes that are living in the cheese. The last of these will be a huge and ever-changing collection of bacteria, yeasts and moulds that find their way into the cheese through the milk, the cheese-making room and equipment and through generally floating about in the air. It is these collections that give different cheeses their unique characteristics, as different groups and concentrations of this microbial flora result in different flavour compounds being released in the breakdown of the cheese.

When I talk about the breakdown of the cheese, I'm not talking about its going mouldy or rotten in the commonly used sense: I mean that the molecules making up the cheese are being changed, being cut up (often resulting in a creamier texture — you can see this as a creamy ring in the interior of a goat's cheese, for example). As I said, different microbes release different by-products and it is these that tend to impart the flavour; but where this gets interesting is that the different microbes all have different preferences for their environments, with reduction, or even complete cessation, of activity when outside their comfort zones. Care must therefore be taken to make sure that the right ones are sufficiently present and that the wrong ones are sufficiently absent.

The *affineur* is tasked with choosing which tastes and textures he wants, and does his best to put the cheese in such an environment that the appropriate flora in the cheese will flourish accordingly. The tools at their disposal are essentially limited to temperature and humidity, but treatments to the rind can also have a big impact on flavour. However, the combinations of these factors are limitless, as are the potential compositions of flora in the cheese to start with.

The *affineur* takes a young cheese and matures it to such a point that it meets the expectations of the people who will buy it. While understanding that working with raw-milk cheeses means uniformity is pretty much impossible, the *affineur* still needs to be able to consistently provide cheeses that will satisfy the needs of the purchaser — and these needs can be quite varied.

For example, the average shop customer will want a cheese that is ready to eat that same evening or at most in a few days' time, but the shop that stocks it will have needed to buy in that cheese earlier so that it can be put on display and gently aged over a period of time in which it will hopefully be purchased.

A restaurant wants great-tasting cheese but it will often have that cheese at an ambient room temperature for long periods of time, so any cheese with the slightest tendency to turn runny becomes very difficult to work with once it has been cut into for the first customer of the evening.

The *affineur* must take all these requirements in hand and at all times age his cheeses to keep the quantity, quality and maturity requirements in check.

The Mons range encompasses a huge number of cheeses of different types, from the young, tangy goat's cheeses and soft Camemberts and Bries, to the pungent washed-rind cheeses and their creamy centres, the smooth, cooked pressed cheeses such as the Comtés and Beauforts, which sit on their shelves in huge wheels with a sort of slightly pompous grandeur, and the blues with their veins of the ubiquitous *Penicillium roqueforti* and salty bite.

I was required to learn how to age each type. Of course, there were numerous differences and peculiarities between the cheeses of a given type, but within that group their treatment, be it rubbing, brushing, washing or simply turning, was broadly the same.

Perhaps my favourite task within the caves was the treatment of the washed-rind cheeses — these are the ones that give cheese its smelly reputation. They tend to have a yellowy orange colour to their rind due to the presence of the humidity-loving *Brevibacterium linens*, the species of bacteria that is associated with unpleasant body odours, particularly around the feet.

As I mentioned earlier, the goal of the *affineur* is to promote changes in the young cheese through promoting certain microbes. What the *B. linens* really requires to flourish is moisture and air. This moisture can be provided by water on its own or other solutions such as diluted vinegar or alcohols. In fact, with French cheeses, there are a large number of examples where the cheeses are washed in a solution of the traditionally produced local alcohol — a classic example of the ever-present regional differences in French food. For example, the Maroille is washed with beer, the Langres in Marc de Champagne and the Epoisses in Marc de Bourgogne. 'Marc' is an alcohol created from the fermentation and distillation of the solid remains of grapes pressed to make wines and champagnes — the same basic idea as grappa.

The obvious question here is: why on earth would anyone go to any trouble at all to take a cheese that *didn't* smell like sweaty feet, and then *make* it smell like sweaty feet? I don't think that I can provide all the answers here, but my understanding is that these cheeses were often historically created as meat substitutes. The flavours of the cheeses are indeed not that far removed from meat partly due to their pleasant bitterness and savoury notes. In addition, it's important not to be too put off by the smell. Although soft, washed-rind cheeses may be aggressive on the nose, they are rarely so brutal with the taste buds. Their gentle but pressing bitterness tends to cut through rich, creamy, and often quite sweet centres, preventing them from cloying on the palate.

The washed-rinds room was awesome. The smell hit you hard enough to make your eyes water. It was small, with movable trolleys, each housing around ten or so shelves. On each of these was a crate full of washed-rind cheeses — Langres, Epoisses, Maroilles and Munsters. The trolleys were covered in white sheets, and, when you peeked inside, the cheeses showed off all the colours of a sunset.

The task of washing the rinds of cheeses

was pleasant but very time-consuming. It involved a small brush and a pot of the appropriate solution for the cheese in question. The cheese was lifted (and in most cases turned over), then brushed gently with the alcohol solution, trying to get into all the wrinkles. The goal was that of moistening, rather than drowning — you looked for an even glisten that said, 'I'm a well-cared-for cheese with great, tasty prospects' rather than the standing pools of liquid on the surface that said, 'In two days' time, mate, I'm going to be an orange puddle.' It's not too difficult to get one of them done right, but when you have literally hundreds to wash before lunch you have to make sure that you aren't rushing and — *quelle horreur!* — using sloppy brushwork.

It may have been for reasons of necessity in terms of the layout of the caves, perhaps to do with plumbing, or not having sufficient space in the main working area, or perhaps it was due to the smell, but, for whatever reason, the washed-rinds room was pretty far removed from the rest of the complex. Washing these cheeses was therefore something of a lonely job, but that was fine: I had a little radio and was more than happy to wash away to the soothing sounds of Nicki Minaj, who seemed to appear on every French radio station at least once every twenty minutes at the time. Sometimes, to keep things interesting, there was even a bit of dancing and singing . . .

★ ★ ★

I wasn't always on my own, however, as, for the most part, I was in the *affineur* group, usually rubbing, turning and sorting the contents of the *hâloir*. On a regular basis, however, we had to tackle the main cave. The main cave in the complex housed the big cheeses and a number of other hangers-on that enjoyed being in the same environment. These cheeses were matured in 'the Tunnel', Hervé's magnificently converted stretch of disused railway tunnel. It was long and damp, and dimly lit. The air there was heady with the mingling scents of different cheeses. The wheels were stored on large boards on shelves in the centre, stacked from floor to ceiling, like priceless relics. Indeed, the Tunnel inspired a sense of almost religious reverence in me the first time I stepped inside. This was my cathedral of cheese, and it made me want to speak in hushed tones for fear of disturbing its ripening inhabitants. The quantity of cheese varied from season to season but was always measured in tens of tonnes. Certainly, there was more there than even the keenest turophile could get through in a lifetime.

The tunnel was a fair trek away from the caves, so the large wheels were stored for the fromagères in what was known as the 'main cave' for dispatch during the week. Given how quickly they went out of the door, they needed relatively little tending. However, the hangers-on — the slightly smaller cheeses that happily shared the same environment as these larger wheels — did need weekly care. These were the Morbiers, Abondances and Taleggios. They were aged in the main cave on large boards, forming shelves that reached up to the ceiling, several metres high.

Morbier is an interesting cheese. Technically, it's pressed and uncooked, but the regular washing of the rind brings out the classic red colours and some of the sharp, almost bitter flavourings associated with a washed-rind cheese — a perfect foil to the otherwise rich and succulent centre.

The cheese weighs around 7 kilos, with a reddish rind and, when cut, a dark line visible running through the centre of its ivory, yellow flesh. Many mistake this line for the *Penicillium* found in blue cheese, but in fact it isn't. Morbier was created when farmers in the Jura had milk left over but insufficient supplies to make a whole new Comté.

Instead, they added rennet and left the milk to coagulate overnight. To protect the cheese and to keep the flies away, the cheese was covered in ash from the fire used to cook the curds in the formation of the Comté. Two of these 'second cheeses' from separate days would then be put together, leaving a line of the ash running through the centre.

Morbier isn't too expensive and melts beautifully when cooked. When tending to a poorly Jen one weekend, who was craving nursery food and feeling very sorry for herself, I discovered it made a fantastic cheese on toast. Cheddar hasn't had a look-in since!

Caring for the Morbiers in the caves meant bringing down a plank's worth (typically three individual cheeses, which would weigh 20–25 kilos, including the plank), turning the cheeses and then brushing them down with a specially concocted solution, made to a secret family recipe. The shelves started at shin height and rose to upstretched-arms-and-tiptoes height, and the work could be quite hard (particularly for feebly muscled accountants).

While I was training with the *affineurs*, I was by no means fast or exceptionally knowledgeable, but I felt as if I was doing well at drinking in the experiences around me and learning how to operate usefully in the team. I was even given my own responsibilities during the morning briefing, although I will admit that, to start with, these were more along the lines of making sure that all the paper-towel dispensers were full. Still, it was progress.

13

It's a Wrap

After a few weeks, my allotted time with the *affineurs* was coming to an end, and so Hervé informed me one Monday morning that it was time for me to join the *fromagères*, or dispatchers. In Lyon I would be performing a similar role to them, albeit with smaller clients. Generally speaking, the caves send cheese to the shops, which then send cheese to restaurants, but the Mons name is carried all the way along the chain so it's important to make sure that the correct controls and standards are in place.

The team of *fromagères* was an interesting one, all female and mostly middle-aged mothers. They were generally very friendly and welcoming, although there were a couple who, while not directly uninviting, wouldn't give me the staff discount on cheeses that I had purchased — even though I'd been there a few months. It wasn't about the money, but it did bring me up short that they still didn't think of me as part of the team.

My training was entrusted to Maryse, who

was short and sharp and ruthlessly organized. No shit was taken, ever, and she upheld high standards — only perfection, swiftly delivered, was good enough. She was the ideal teacher, although she was at times rather intimidating. Her yells of '*Matt, viens me voir!*' (Matt, come and see me!) induced a level of workplace fear that I had never encountered before.

To start out, I work-shadowed one of the *fromagères*, learning to read the orders that came in, how to use the systems for weighing, recording and creating usage-date stickers. The most important aspect was learning to pick the right cheeses. There were plenty of different *affinages* to choose from, and each client had their foibles. It took me a little while to get the hang of this, but, thankfully by this point, I had a good grounding in the work that the *affineurs* were doing, so I was able to recognize how ripe and ready a cheese was, usually just by eye.

We would take a tour of the caves with a large rolling table to select the required quantities of the cheeses before heading back to the workstation to weigh and wrap them before crating them up. Sounds simple, but speed and accuracy were important and, without some serious organization, you found yourself with a groaning mountain of cheese and very little space to deal with it — a situation shortly followed by a ticking off from Maryse.

I learned the system, with some help, and before long I was being given my own small orders to deal with. One of our international clients liked to receive prepacked boxes of Mons-wrapped cheeses, which they would then sell on to *their* clients. The contents of the different types of boxes had been agreed long in advance and the client simply sent through an order for, say, ten boxes of seven cheeses and fifteen boxes of five cheeses.

This was a great exercise for someone in training like me as the weight of each cheese needed to be precise to avoid making a loss by sending too much or risk displeasing the client by sending too little cheese. On top of this, I was required to cut neatly and select cheeses of the correct *affinage* to survive the journey. Finally, wrapping up the cheeses had to be done neatly and efficiently before making sure that each box contained the correct selection.

I have a personal tendency towards perfectionism, a frustrating trait because it means that I am rarely happy with the work that I produce — but here I was able to perfect my wrapping, organization and cutting, creating tidy rows of identically wrapped cheeses before slotting each neatly into its box just so. It satisfied me on a weird obsessive-compulsive level. However, therein lay a problem.

I found quite quickly that I had hit a bit of a stumbling block: simply put, I had difficulty meeting the requirement to move fast for sustained periods of time. At the time I was justifying it to myself as the result of a conversation with Hervé over Christmas, when I was aware that I had been going a little slowly. He told me that I shouldn't be asking if I was working fast enough, but whether I was working well enough. The perfectionist within me latched onto this snippet and I was living by it. That was a mistake.

You can get away with that kind of behaviour in an environment like this for a day or two, but not for weeks. I remembered a cautionary email during my initial correspondence with Mons the previous year: 'We can't afford to take on someone who walks fast when the rest of the team is running.'

I wasn't even walking fast. The worst of it was that people had noticed and were commenting on it. It was meant as encouragement, but it hurt to hear it.

I made it my goal to get faster, to stop second-guessing and to just bloody get on with it. I had to match the speed of the others or I could never hope to be considered anything other than a tourist — I think, at the heart of it, I was starting to worry that I might be just that.

For most tasks I would ask how long it should take and time myself. I would clock-watch, race others and try to hone my movements through the caves to be more efficient. I worked hard at this, really hard.

Did it help?

Yes, thankfully. I saw my speed improve, but I was still never fast, just less embarrassingly slow. I don't move that way, I never have and I probably never will. I decided at that point that, though speed was important, I would have to differentiate myself through quality of work — but always, of course, with a nod towards zippiness.

★ ★ ★

Weeks had passed and I was still working with the *fromagères*, often on the boxes. I was halfway through a large batch and my timing was going OK — well, I hadn't drawn any ire from Maryse, so it can't have been going too badly.

I was taking a coffee break with Collette, a good-natured, slightly matronly member of the *fromagère* team, making idle chitchat in the reception room. Hervé passed through, wearing his Mons baseball cap, work coat and most business-like expression. I hadn't seen much of him over the recent week due to various important cheese missions he had been undertaking throughout the country, visiting producers and sourcing potential new cheeses for the Mons range.

'How's the work going?' he asked, in a brisk Auvergnat flurry.

'Good, thanks,' we responded, I more stiltedly than Collette.

'So, is Matt getting on OK?' He was still on the move as he said this, and practically shot it backwards over his shoulder.

'Oh, fine, sometimes we have difficulty understanding him, though, but we all make an effort and usually we get to the bottom of what he's trying to say,' Collette responded with a small smirk. Ouch!

Hervé did little more than slow his pace slightly on his way out of the room upon hearing this comment, but I knew immediately that I would be hearing more about it from him in our next meeting. It was particularly frustrating because I really didn't know where this comment had come from — I had thought that the hard work of learning to make myself understood was over, but suddenly it felt like a whole new and rather steep incline on this cheese mountain that I had to overcome.

Sure enough, I received my summons to Hervé's office later that day. He beckoned me in and to sit down while he finished his phone call. There was a notepad (Mons-branded, but of course!) and pen on the desk.

'Matt, this is a test,' he said. 'When you're in Lyon, you're going to need to be able to take cheese orders over the phone.' His attention firmly shifted to me as he peered at me over his glasses. 'I want you to write down the weights and names of these cheeses that I read out.'

He proceeded to rattle through a list of cheeses and I wrote them down. There was no problem there. I was pretty confident with the Mons range by that point and I had been around Hervé enough to be accustomed to his accent. He was happy with my performance. Cue a big sigh of relief — the crisis was averted, for now.

Then, he started asking me questions about the cheeses in the Mons range. I stumbled over some pretty obvious ones, about the type of milk used, how they were made and, importantly, where. I realized that I had overlooked something pretty important. I knew what the cheeses looked like, where to find them and how to judge their *affinage*, but that was where it ended. I didn't know where they were from, or much about how the farmers went about making them.

A crucial difference between my role in the caves and my future in the shop was that, in the shop, I would be communicating with clients. In the caves, I had never had to describe or sell a cheese.

Hervé took a deep breath. 'With an obvious English accent like yours, you will *have* to know significantly more about what you're selling than the client; you will have to shock them with your understanding and expertise for them to take you seriously. You need to know where the cheese was made, down to the names of the next-door neighbours and each of the cattle.'

A follow-up test was booked in for the next week, and in the seven days that followed I had to learn everything about the French AOC cheeses, of which there are almost fifty.

Hang on. AOC?

The AOC cheeses are massively important. AOC stands for Appellation d'Origine Contrôlée (or controlled designation of origin) and is a label applied to certain cheeses (and many other artisanal or farmhouse produce, including vegetables, fruit, wines, spirits and meat). It is a legally controlled label that confirms the product has abided by a set of rules designed to protect both the traditional production methods and the geographical link to the product. A well-known example of the AOC system in action is that champagne can be produced in only one specific area of France; produced elsewhere by the same method, it must be sold under a different name.

To obtain the protection, a given product must go through a rather bureaucratic process to firmly establish the presence of a substantive link between the unique qualities of a product and the *terroir*, or geographic area, from which it is created and then to detail the traditional methodology that makes the product unique.

For the right to put the label on his produce, a producer must meet all of the requirements of the agreed methodology. These rules are enforced by the French government through the organization that regulates agricultural products that have protected designations of origin, the Institut National de l'Origine et de la Qualité (INAO). Importantly, the INAO also enforces the restriction on producers using the label when they don't meet the requirements.

This is important for the consumer, who, when buying their Camembert de Normandie, can be assured that it has been made in Normandy following the agreed methodology. They will thus be safe in the knowledge that it was not made in Sevenoaks with dog milk.

The first cheese to be protected under the AOC label was Roquefort in 1925, which already had something of a history of protectionism dating from the fifteenth century, when the citizens of the commune Roquefort-sur-Soulzon were granted a monopoly on the ageing of the cheese in their unique caves.

Obviously, being graced with the AOC label will add a value to a given product. Therefore, it is unsurprising that there are significant financial incentives at play for those in the cheese industry, be they new entrants or experienced producers. The rules behind the AOC labels can be changed, however, and there was a nasty spat in 2007, when the big industrial players in Camembert production sought a change to the AOC rules allowing the milk to be heat-treated. The INAO refused this change and Camembert de Normandie remains 100 per cent *lait cru*, or raw milk. However, you will still find many cheeses called 'Camembert' in the shops, but, if it doesn't bear the exact name 'Camembert de Normandie,' then it doesn't have to meet the AOC guidelines.

I believe that, without this system, there are a number of cheeses that might not have survived, making it a great success. However, you should know that the label in itself does not guarantee a top-quality farmhouse or artisan cheese. For that, you need to talk to your cheesemonger — and I don't mean the one under the bright antiseptic lights of the supermarket.

OK, sorry, one final point. AOC is, or rather was, the French system. This was overtaken by the European-wide Appellation d'Origine Protégée (AOP) label in the trailing end of the last decade. Almost all qualifying French AOC cheeses have attained AOP status, the only exception to my knowledge, as of early 2013, being the Rigotte de Condrieu, which at the time of writing was still sold under the AOC label.

★ ★ ★

The test that Hervé had set up for me would require me to be able to reel off information about production and *terroir* for any one of the forty-five French AOC cheeses. That represented a lot of information, and I wasn't quite sure how deep Hervé wanted me to go. Would the village in which the farm was located be enough to appease him, or would I really have had to have learned the names of each of the respective herds' key milkers, plus, probably, what the farmer and his wife enjoyed eating for breakfast? It was certainly a challenge, but I had fun making coded maps of France and giving myself a crash course in the geography of cheese. My general understanding of French geography benefited enormously, too.

Before that meeting with Hervé, I hadn't truly grasped the extra challenges that my Englishness would pose for me when I was working in French cheese. I was determined to prove myself, and, thankfully, the test was passed without incident. Hervé gave me a brief pat on the shoulder as I returned to the caves and the team of *fromagères*. It was probably intended as encouragement, but I couldn't help feeling that it meant, 'I'm watching you, *Anglais*.'

14

Montbrison

My training continued, and then, almost before I knew it, May had rolled into June and I still hadn't started at the shop.

I'm not going to lie. I was getting a bit frustrated and also concerned that, with summer coming up, I might start looking like a prime candidate for providing cheap holiday cover. I took the plunge and voiced my concern to Hervé, looking for some renewed assurance that my training might soon be over.

He let me know that they were certainly intending to employ me, but that I would have to wait a few more weeks. It was pretty much the response that I was expecting, so I had prepared a proposition: I put it to Hervé that, although I had been gaining lots of great experience in maturing cheese — looking after cheeses, rubbing cheeses, cutting cheeses, wrapping up and sending cheeses — I didn't have any experience in selling cheese to customers, and, given that I was going to be working in a shop, it might be a good idea to get some shop experience before starting in Lyon. I will admit that I was hoping this might kick-start my return to Lyon and getting my foot in the door in the shop in Les Halles.

Hervé had other ideas. A few days later he called me into his office to tell me he had arranged for me to work at the Mons shop in Montbrison, a pretty town about an hour south of the caves, for three weekends before starting at Lyon.

The Mons shop in Montbrison was run by Cédric Lenoir, whom I already knew from the caves, although I had rarely had an extended conversation with him. He would visit most weeks to check on all the cheese that the caves had to offer and he would select and reserve the ones that suited him well. He wasn't alone in doing this, of course: many of the other shop owners could be found exploring the caves in the hopes of unearthing hidden treasures.

Cédric was intense and incredibly serious about cheese, well versed in its lore and main characters. He was wiry and lean, with dark eyes that darted about like a bird's as he talked. He spoke in a clipped and precise tone, and, while friendly, his comments were sometimes acerbic and presented with a self-belief that one could easily imagine had been well earned.

We had a meeting in Hervé's office and it was settled. I would be starting the following weekend, working in the shop on Friday and Saturday. Cédric would also help me to arrange a morning on a local farm, in fact the only one left making the famous local blue cheese, Fourme de Montbrison.

The following Friday morning I left the caves with Cédric's order: my car boot was filled with cheese, and a box of two hundred eggs sat on the passenger seat. I entered Montbrison town centre into the satnav and drove out into the countryside of the Loire. Summer had clearly hit — you could smell it. The air was warm, the sky was blue and bees droned lazily among the roadside flowers. I wound down the windows for a bit of a breeze and put on my newly repurchased copy of Jurassic 5's awesome first album. I had (tragically) lost my old one somewhere between Durham and London. Jen might disagree, but for me it's about as good as summertime driving music gets.

I pulled up in the town centre; it was picture-book pretty, with pots of bright flowers in the corners of the town square, cobbled streets and people stopping to chat and laugh in the sunshine, or reading the morning paper at a pavement café with an espresso or a refreshing *citron pressé*.

The shop was well situated on a corner right in the heart of the town, although thankfully set back a little from the market square. I pulled up outside, unloaded the cheese and eggs and headed in to meet Cédric and his team before getting ready for some serious cheese selling (dressed smartly of course in my freshly ironed, Mons-branded white shirt and Mons-branded brown apron).

The shop was spotless and elegant, if petite. The cheese looked great. It was one of the first times that I had had the chance to really study cheeses *on sale*. Effectively, at the caves, the cheese had already been sold. This was a ground-breaking paradigm shift for me. To others, I suspect less so, but bear with me and I'll try to explain.

As an *affineur*, you're essentially in the position of a parent. You may not see the child, sorry, *cheese*, being born, but you are enormously important in its life from a very early age. You shape its future through care and affection, helping it to be the best it can be, letting it have the fruitful and tasty life that it deserves. But then the cheese is packed up and sent away, and, hard as it may be, the *affineur* must move on to help raise more cheeses through their difficult teenage years (or weeks or days) before they too are sent out into the world.

Actually, the *affineur* is probably closer to the boarding school house tutor, or the governess. That would make the parent the farmer. Thinking about it, if it's hard for the *affineur* it must be worse still for the farmer, letting your child, sorry, *cheese*, be raised and matured in someone else's care.

The metaphor is, I'll admit, rather laboured, but the point I'm driving at is that the cheese looks probably the best that it ever will in the shop. This is its first big job interview, its wedding day. Professional care has been taken to make it handsome and appealing in the shop window.

Actually, this process of putting cheese on display is rather more complicated than it might initially seem. It's a kind of 'cheese shop theory', and Cédric was a fervent believer in this ever-evolving set of rules.

I have since learned the massive impact that the positioning of cheese has on the quantities sold. People gravitate towards certain positions in the display with astonishing frequency, almost regardless of the cheeses put there. But, of course, with great power comes great mongering responsibility: if you sell a crap cheese by virtue of craftily chosen prime positioning, that customer isn't going to be happy when they come to tuck into their purchase. At best you'll get your ear bent the next time they come in; at worst, they'll never come back.

There are just so many important decisions to be made. For instance, do you put cheeses of a given type together — maybe all the goat's cheeses, or all of the pungent, orange, washed-rind cheese such as Epoisses, Langres and Maroilles? If you do, you can easily offer a client a choice for a given style, but mixing up the cheese types allows you to offer a choice of cheese type instead. The customer might not choose that particular example in front of them, but seeing the different types in proximity helps in their visualization of a cheese board.

You can also organize by size, giving your shop its own geography: mountainous ranges of cooked alpine cheeses such as the Comtés and Beauforts, descending into the rolling hills of pressed cheeses such as Saint-Nectaire and Tomme de Savoie, and the low-lying grassy plains of the goat's cheese and softer cow's-milk cheeses, then rising again into a smaller outcrop of blue cheeses that overlook a lake of fresh cheeses, glistening whitely under the flattering lights of the display.

How do you present your cheeses? A cut cheese open to the air looks great for a while, but if the atmosphere is hot and dry it will soon fissure, sweat, droop or turn into a puddle. If you film your cheeses you risk giving your shop that shiny supermarket look, or, worse, you look scruffy with loose ends of film dangling about.

Do you pre-cut your cheeses to save time and create a nice display, letting the customer choose the piece that appeals to them, or do you cut from the block, reducing the opportunity for small pieces to dry out?

What is your shop's approach to cutting cheeses? There are many accepted styles for cutting certain cheeses. For example, the cylindrical Fourme d'Ambert has perhaps three acceptable methods of cutting: equally into eighths by virtue of one horizontal and two vertical cuts; sliced horizontally with the rinds at the cylinder's ends discarded; or with a couple of slices taken out of the middle and the ends each cut into four equal pieces. A minefield.

I suppose that these questions don't necessarily have universally correct answers, just the most *appropriate* answers for a given shop's style, location and clientele.

Cédric had his own answers. They had been well considered and clearly proven to work. Since opening in 2006 he had essentially dominated the cheese market in Montbrison, his confrères having hung up their cheese wires in the face of too stiff a competition.

He was a stickler for detail, often asking me to refilm a piece of cheese several times to get it just right or rewrap a cut piece of cheese more neatly, or he'd comment on a better way to handle a cheese knife. He'd imbued this understanding of 'good practice' in his staff and they placed the same enormous emphasis on the presentation and quality of the cheeses that they sell as he did.

I remember the wide-eyed look of shock followed by, 'Good God, don't let Cédric see you handle cheese like that!' as I slid a line of several little discs of Picodon across the display by what could have been no more than a few centimetres to make room for a larger cheese. 'You pick them up and move them one at a time.'

That first day was hard: my French had never been tested on paying customers before and, while I had a lot of experience cutting and wrapping cheeses, the pieces that I was selling in the shop just weren't quite the same narrow-angled points or, the most difficult of all, obtuse angles. It took me most of the morning to get the hang of these new cuts and folds, but by the afternoon I was pretty happy with them. Thankfully, the weather was hot and the few customers in town were happy to idle in the cool of the shop while I was learning the ropes.

The other major shock to me was dealing with money. I, as we all do, buy things on a daily basis, but counting out change if you've never done it before can be a bit fraught at times. Without a clear process in your head, the arithmetic can get a bit sketchy, particularly if it's a moving target, with people offering different amounts of small change when you're halfway through counting up.

If I'm honest, I found that first day pretty tough. I was massively stressed and quite happy for people not to come into the shop at all. Just keep walking and don't come in to see me embarrass myself, I willed to the passers-by.

* * *

After my first day in the shop I returned to Lyon tired and with quite mixed feelings about how I'd got on. Jen and I were planning on an evening out before I headed back to Montbrison for the Saturday. Continuing our quest to try as many different restaurants as possible in a city with almost two thousand to choose from, we went out for dinner. Unfortunately, the subsequent pain has made me forget exactly what we ordered, but I'm sure it was lovely.

Heading home to our little flat on the Métro, I was too involved in my phone to competently descend the steps. It was hardly a dramatic fall, but it resulted in searing pain in my right ankle and the inability to put any weight on it. Jen, noticing that I had gone a zombie-like shade of pale grey and was trying not to faint, managed to coerce a burly Frenchman into helping me to the assistance point, where, thankfully, there was a chair. The service staff at the Bellecour Métro station were awesome — friendly, very helpful but also quite mocking in a sort of gentle way: 'Normally people are more drunk than you before they throw themselves down our stairs.'

A trip to the doctor the next day confirmed that there were no breaks, just a vicious sprain. My foot was spectacularly blue and very swollen, and I was on crutches for a few days, before progressing to an ankle support. It's amazing what a hindrance a sprained ankle can be when your work involves a lot of driving and mainly standing up and lifting things all day.

Cédric was very understanding when I called him, but, nonetheless, I felt like an idiot. Now I had even more work to do before I could prove myself as anything more than a bumbling and evidently clumsy Englishman.

★ ★ ★

The following week, I was due to spend the day making Fourme de Montbrison at the farm run by Marie-Agnès and René Plagne. My foot wasn't in great shape, but I'd had the OK from the doctor that driving was safe and I was not about to miss this opportunity.

Fourme de Montbrison is one of the less well-known French AOP cheeses. It's a cow's-milk blue that comes in a cylindrical shape weighing about 2 kilos. Its rind is a beautiful orangey golden colour with a sweet, fermented smell that leaves a lingering musty and woody odour — this comes from ageing the cheeses on gutter-shaped spruce planks. The centre of the cheese is a rich ivory colour with a fine, dry and crumbling texture, marbled with delicate veins of blue (that same *Penicillium roqueforti* that derives its name from its first use, in the production of Roquefort).

The name *fourme* apparently derives from the Greek *formos*, which represented the recipient in which curds were shaped into cheeses. From this route came the old French *fourmage*, which over time evolved into the word *fromage*, meaning cheese in modern French. The term *fourme* is now applied to French cheeses of a rather specific cylindrical shape including Fourme d'Ambert, made just across the border into the Auvergne.

In flavour, Fourme de Montbrison is surprisingly mild, quite milky with a faint woodiness. There's definitely an element from the blue mould, but it's mild, lacking the spicy piquancy of some other classic blues such as Roquefort and Stilton.

At that time there were only three producers of this cheese in France, one fairly large-scale producer, one artisanal, and one farmhouse: the Plagnes.

This situation was bordering on precarious, putting the farm-made version of the cheese on the 'endangered species' list, with the risk that within the next couple of decades there may no longer be a farmhouse-produced Fourme de Montbrison anywhere in the world. In fact, this had already happened when the previous generation of farmers eschewed its production, leaving supply to those who bought in milk. The Plagnes worked hard to recreate the original character of the cheese, one that can trace its origins back to the Middle Ages, made on the Monts de Forez in chalets for the historical markets of Ambert and Montbrison either side of what is now the dividing line between the Auvergne and the Rhône-Alpes regions.

When they retire, who knows if someone

will pick up the mantle again?

Now I should point out that the other versions of the cheese are still good, even excellent. There is nothing wrong with them *per se*. It's just that for me the tradition of the cheese seemed to be tied closely to the farmer with his animals, making cheese up in those mountain pastures. Perhaps I'm wrong here, but for me the maintenance of that close link between animal and production is a tradition worth celebrating (above and beyond the quality of the cheese itself).

In 2013, two new producers were judged worthy of making Fourme de Montbrison under the AOP stamp, which was great news, although these are not farmhouse productions.

The Fourme de Montbrison is a good example of the difficulties felt with French farmhouse cheese, and, while on a subconscious level I had been aware of the problem, it wasn't until I was out actually talking to the farmers that I truly realized how precarious their position was.

René is the eighth generation of farmers producing this cheese (with a gap where his parents stopped making it), and, while he and his wife are passionate and motivated, they aren't getting younger and their three children look unlikely to take up the reins.

They will most likely sell their farm. I fervently hope that someone keen to maintain the tradition will purchase it.

When driving to the Plagne farm I passed La Fromagerie du Pont de la Pierre, the largest and most industrial of those three remaining Fourme de Montbrison manufacturers. This *fromagerie* produced a pasteurized cheese that, while good to the taste, to my mind lacks the complexity and finish of the raw-milk versions. It is, however, cheaper than the artisanal and *fermier* versions and it is therefore not hard to see its appeal.

However, Marie-Agnès and René compete on quality, and here they do well. A considerable proportion of their output is purchased by Mons and distributed to the Mons shops. Unsurprisingly, a large quantity is delivered by René directly to the shop in Montbrison.

The cheese-making process for Fourme de Montbrison is no laughing matter. The large vat containing several hundred litres of gently warmed milk is seeded with the *Penicillium roqueforti* and undergoes a relatively fast rennet coagulation. During this process, there is little visual change, but this belies the complex macromolecular adjustments that are going on with the de-knitting and re-knitting of proteins to form the curd, almost like a milk jelly.

I am told to keep my distance from the vat to make sure that vibrations don't fissure the gel. Marie-Agnès judges the set by eye and by touch, inserting a finger at an angle and bringing it to the surface to see how it splits. This is a common action in cheese making, and it took me right back to making Tommes with Bruno.

Once it is set, a lengthy process of cutting and stirring is undertaken to ensure that the correct grain size is reached, and that sufficient liquid is removed from the curd. A newly set curd is a bit like a three-dimensional net, with liquid (water or whey) in the gaps. When you cut through it, the enclosed liquid can escape, and the more you cut, the more can escape. Similarly, stirring the curds agitates them, releasing further water, as does heating, which can cause the proteins to contract, squeezing out the trapped liquids.

Once the curds are the right size, the residual whey is partially drained from the vat, making it easier to extract the solid matter with a bucket. The curds clump together in the vat as they are left to rest before we fish them out, drain them off and break them up into crumbs by hand, with a good dose of salt. The breaking-up of the lumps is done in a specific pattern to ensure that all of the curd is worked the same amount before the cheeses are put into the moulds.

The quantity of curd in each mould was carefully eyed by Marie-Agnès: too little or too much and the cheese might not meet the strict weight and height requirements of the AOP rules, and consistent failings in this respect could cause the farm to lose its right to label the cheese 'Fourme de Montbrison'.

The *fourmes* are left to drip under their own weight and are turned from time to time prior to their placement in the spruce guttering. Pressure is not used to force out more liquid with this cheese.

At this point, the cheese will remain pale yellow in the centre, and, though the spores of the *Penicillium* are present, they will not grow, because they require oxygen to do so. Oxygen is introduced into the centre of the cheese once it's aged a little, to ensure that the right balance of flavour and texture is acquired. Small holes are made by long needles in the form of an evil-looking comb. The same process is used for almost all blue cheeses.

Once we had finished washing up and mopping down, we headed to the farm kitchen for lunch. I've always thought that farm kitchens seem to have their own style: generally warm and welcoming, where business and family life collide. My forearms were still burning from the enthusiastic crumbling that I'd been doing but the discomfort soon slipped my mind as Marie-Agnès put together the perfect lunch for the adventuring cheese lover: slices of Fourme on toast, gently grilled until bubbling and starting to brown, followed by pasta with a rich Fourme and cream sauce and thin slices of rare steak. This was hearty food, perfect after a morning's work.

I asked her why it was so difficult to make raw-milk cheeses, and she said it was because the milk was alive and never behaved the same way twice. She said that she could tell when René had had a tough day milking or was in a bad mood, because the curd wouldn't gel in the same way, potentially to do with stress hormones in the cow's milk as they pick up on the farmer's anxiety. Even if Marie-Agnès had been exaggerating slightly about the level of the connection between her husband and his cattle, it was still very clear that the link between animal husbandry and cheese production was very strong here.

As I drove off, I reflected that I was happy to have met such inspiring people, to have been a part of the production, to have broken bread with them and to have been taken seriously as part of the industry.

I was also happy to have the weight off my still purplish foot.

★ ★ ★

The very next day I was back in the Montbrison shop, armed with new knowledge on their most frequently sold product. I was able to chat the chat and the whole process made a lot more sense. I let go a bit, and managed to find my way back to what I love doing: talking about cheese. I was explaining why the customers should take this one or that one, what to drink with it and how much they needed. I'd been learning this sort of stuff at the caves, but before that day in the shop it was as if there were a stopper in my brain preventing me from applying what I'd learned.

The Friday passed quite slowly again, with relatively few clients, but I was learning the movements of the shop: when to clean the knives, how to judge smoking breaks, which cheeses needed filming and when. I was starting to feel like an extra pair of hands, rather than a hindrance.

Saturday, however, was great. I had a brilliant time, feeling comfortable with the work and the shop style. I'm not going to pretend that I was great — I was a bit stilted at times and sometimes struggled to communicate effectively with the clients — but I managed to sell cheese while looking professional, not foolish, as I had feared.

Not even the bright-green parking ticket that greeted me on my return to my car could dampen my spirits. I may only have been starting to scratch the surface of the cheese world, but the deeper I went, the more I loved it.

15

Two Departures

Things were finally slotting into place. I still had my problems, speediness being the most obvious of them, but I really felt that I had enough under my belt to hit the ground running in Lyon. My experiences in Montbrison had shown me that working in a shop was really just an extension of what I was doing in the caves, the cheeses were the same, as was the cutting and wrapping. The only difference was that there was someone standing there asking you questions. But hey, I like talking about cheese, so that was all to the good.

I was still in the caves, however, and this was in part due to the sad passing of a true hero in the cheese world, Hubert Mons, the father of Hervé and Laurent. He was a great man, and responsible for setting his sons on the path to creating the organization that Mons is today. His activity in the business had clearly diminished, but his presence was still felt. The caves were in mourning.

I certainly didn't blame anyone for not having time to look into my transfer to Lyon while organizing a funeral.

* * *

In these final weeks, I had been flitting
between the teams, sometimes with the
affineurs, sometimes with the fromagères.

I remember taking charge of the washed
rinds for the morning, washing the Maroilles
and Langres. For once, I had company in the
pungent washed-rinds room. Nat, one of the
other affineurs, had come to join me. Nat had
one of those faces that change completely
when their owners smile — and she did so
frequently. She had ruddy cheeks and glasses
that she used to take off and polish every five
minutes, and was always there to help out the
rest of the team. That morning we'd got into
a comfortable rhythm together, dipping and
brushing in time with each other (and, of
course, in time with the dulcet tones of Nicki
Minaj in the background).

Suddenly, she stopped, and placed the
brush deliberately back into her little pot. 'Do
you know what, Matt?' she said. 'We're going
to miss you around here.'

I looked over at her and grinned.

'I mean, sure, you're not the fastest, but
you get it. You love these cheeses,' she
continued, gesturing fondly around her at the

crates of our wrinkly, yellow wards, 'and I trust that you know what's best for them. We all do.'

I could have kissed her! It was immeasurably gratifying to hear that my hard work had been paying off. Instead, I gave her a heartfelt 'Merci' and finished brushing my Langres with a bit of a flourish.

Things had been going better with the fromagères, too. I had been working hard on my speed, and on good days I could now very nearly match the team with my wrapping, cutting and folding. I would generally be given my own orders to take to start from finish and from time to time helped out with the training of other interns, spending time in the Villa and caves.

Alain approached me, asking if I wanted to try my hand at cutting open a Parmesan, solo. Of course, I was keen. It had been a while since I had last tried, and failed, and since then I had been regularly opening wheels of Comté, Beaufort and Gruyère for the fromagères. I was leaner and meaner, and this time I was going to show the world that I had some cheese chops.

I won't pretend that I was lightning fast, or that I ended up looking like anything other than a sweaty beetroot, but the Parmesan was cut into two respectably equal halves and I was very satisfied with myself. In fact, I kept the metal badge from that wheel of cheese that the Italian *affineur* would hammer into everything that he matured. It is now mounted in a photo frame on the mantelpiece as a physical reminder of the fact that I had made a clearly evidenced improvement in my technical ability.

★   ★   ★

I knew I was leaving. I just wasn't sure when. I could feel myself disengaging, and looking forward rather than focusing on the here and now. Over the last few weeks I had been sharing the Villa with Victor, an enthusiastic food lover with a luxuriant moustache. He had been living in Australia with his wife, a pastry chef named Vy, and had returned to his native France to learn as much as possible from Hervé and the Mons team. He shared my passion about cheese, and his ability to talk at length about it, sometimes without appearing to draw breath, was impressive. The team at the caves were immediately fond of him, although I had once caught Maryse hissing behind her hand, 'He just doesn't. Stop. Talking!'

Before long, Hervé had decided that Victor and I should be sent to the Lyon shop at around the same time, and I was excited at the prospect of joining the team with such a kindred foodie spirit. Guillaume was soon to be moving on to pastures new, so the Lyon team were looking for as much new meat as possible. As our time in the caves drew to an end, Victor hit some last-minute visa issues, and had to return to Australia for a few weeks, setting back his Lyon start date.

We spent a final evening together at the Villa: marinated and barbecued chicken with homemade baps, salad, cheese (naturally) and a fair amount of beer. It was a summer's evening, and it was full of promise. It really felt as if we had been trained up to be part of a change in the shop. It was exhilarating.

The following morning, I drove Victor back to Lyon and we visited Les Halles, and Etienne. He, smiling as ever, was genuinely pleased to see us, despite its being a Saturday morning and therefore pretty hectic. We chatted about the future and Les Halles in general and I showed Victor around the shop, before pointing out some of the other well-respected shops. We had a simple, but solid, meal at a bar, followed by a Saint-Marcellin from La Mère Richard, our major competition in Lyon.

We went our separate ways, he to Australia and I back to the flat to prepare for Jen's arrival — she had been back to London for work and was due in that evening.

★ ★ ★

My last day in the caves was not quite how I had imagined it would be. I had arrived at the Villa the evening before and was prepared for my final week. I had my list of final questions to ask, a vague idea of some photos that I would like to take and a sense of excitement that I really was about to become a genuine, paid cheesemonger.

In the briefing it had been decided that I would be working with Alain on departures and 'large wheels,' and there I was, breaking down Comtés, when Isabelle, the accountant, spotted me on her way to the office. She looked rather confused and asked me what I was doing there. It turns out that the email sent around to everyone to confirm my start date at the shop had not been updated to take into account the most recent extension to my internship and that my contract started on Tuesday, the following day.

I explained the situation to Hervé, making it clear that I knew we had agreed on the following week and would certainly honour that, but, of course, if my presence was really required in the shop, I would be able to drop

218

everything and head back to Lyon that evening.

Hervé said that I should go. He said that I was ready.

16

Talking Shop

With the stress of the scramble to pack up the Villa, leave and drive back the night before, I was feeling a little groggy as I left the flat and made my way to the shop. The sun had made it out of bed before I had, brightly lighting Lyon's empty morning streets. But, by the time I was at Les Halles, I was alert, although ready for another coffee.

Etienne was in the small office, checking his emails, and greeted me with a big smile and a handshake. He offered a uniform, but I had already stocked up well before leaving the caves. Nicely pressed shirt and apron? Check!

As I made my way down to the shop, Guillaume and Sabrina were already starting to prepare the display. After the weekend rush, the cheeses would all be carefully wrapped up and left in the humid cave while the shop received a thorough clean. On Tuesdays, when the cheesemongering week starts, we took stock of the cheeses that we needed to push, any new arrivals or any weekly promotions that we might be running, and we set up the display accordingly, starting from a blank canvas. This is now one of my favourite parts of the job: you craft the *ambiance* of the shop for the week, setting the scene as you lay out your wares.

As I smiled and said '*bonjour*', I received a nearly identical pair of frosty stares. I had of course been aware that my presence would probably be seen as an unwanted element of change. It was difficult seeing it in their eyes, though — clearly I had some work to do on my team bonding.

The first task was to organize the cheese into neat rows, grouping generally in terms of hard cheeses, goat's milk cheeses, fresh cheeses, soft cheeses and finally the *tommes* and *raclette* cheeses. These categories had more or less fixed positions, otherwise the clients would get confused, but within those positions we had free rein. We knew that there were 'quiet' areas in the display that people tended to gravitate away from for unknown mystical reasons, so we tended to make sure that these were filled with the big hitters that everyone would ask for, such as Camembert and Brie.

Once the cheeses were laid out, we started on the decoration and general prettifying of the shop: small fern leaves were added as a rich contrast between the dark-brown wood and the pale colours of the cheeses, the windows were wiped down, removing the sticky fingerprints of eager clients. We buffed and polished and made sure that the *mise en place* was, er, put in place. A fridge full of Saint-Marcellins was wrapped and ready to go; spare points of the most popular hard cheeses were kept in the wings and salad and bread were prepared for clients coming to taste cheese at the bar.

I was expecting to be shown the ropes, how the tills worked and the general methodology for the shop, but everyone was busy doing their own thing, and largely left me to get on with it. In the shop, the education was not delivered in a chunk but infused over the weeks and months, largely without verbal cues. This was something of a shock to me when I first started.

I was lost in the middle of the set-up when I noticed a client in front of me. I hadn't been shown how to use the multicoloured, many-buttoned interface of the till but I felt that I couldn't really pass the buck, as others were busy. I had a short discussion with the client about what she was after; we selected some suitable cheeses, which I cut up and wrapped neatly; then I bodged the order through the till.

That was it, no fanfare, just a happy

customer, and now I understood how the till worked. I had professionally mongered my first cheese. I realized that in my head I had built the complexity of the process up into completely unrealistic proportions.

★　★　★

I quickly came to understand that, really, there was nothing outrageously complicated about working in or running a shop. The difficulty lay in keeping on top of the details, and these were legion, from the act of creating a display, organizing a cleaner, remembering who you had to call when the grating machine broke down, to basics such as working cleanly and making sure that there was change in the till. When working, it was important to always try to view the shop from a customer's perspective, keeping things neat and tidy, cheeses well ordered, labels neatly aligned, surfaces wiped down and sales patter appropriate for the situation.

I soon came under fire for being just a little too chatty with the customers. I couldn't help it. I just loved talking about cheese and these people were interested. For me this was a revelation. I have never been the one to stand up and present, to seek interactions with clients. I'd always been happy in support roles.

Of course, this was a business and I was a paid employee, so I had to fall in line and find a way to cut down my chatter politely, while still providing a good level of guidance. It's a difficult balance to find and one that has to be constantly adjusted according to the number of clients in front of you.

In general, the customers to our shop were friendly and polite. However, it was clear that the fact that I was English set me apart, and coloured nearly all of my interactions, both positively and negatively. My French was certainly good enough for the job in hand and I rarely had a problem in communicating, but my accent would never allow me to pass as a Frenchman.

The problem was that there were a considerable number of French people who maintained the belief that France made the best cheese and that anything foreign should be avoided at all costs. There were a few who took this further and specifically singled out the UK as a gastronomic wasteland.

I remember an occasion when a smartly dressed, very *proper* lady, with tightly permed hair and a coat made of what looked like real fur who had been looking at the display, asked me to explain the differences between the three different Comtés that we stocked.

'Of course, madam,' I started, about to

launch into a well-practised, concise description of the key difference: the maturity of the cheese, and how that impacted on flavour and texture, and of course price. I didn't get the chance to finish, however, as my initial comment was met with, 'Oh, you're English: it's clear that I won't be getting good advice here, then,' in a rather shrill and haughty voice as she walked off without a goodbye.

I was pretty angry about that, and did my best to keep my cool. Thankfully, such forthright commentators were rare. That said, I did have to deal with around one in four of my customers pointing out the fact that I was English and 'Isn't it funny that you are selling cheese in France?' At the beginning of my time with Etienne, I agreed, it seemed very funny.

These comments didn't stop, though, and, while they weren't necessarily meant with malice or concern, I did find them draining. I wanted the conversation to be about the cheese, not my country of origin. A good example of this in action was that a number of clients would approach Etienne and say something like, 'Your Englishman over there, he sold me a cheese the other day. Well, we were very pleasantly surprised to find that it was actually nice!'

Rather than let myself get too depressed

about this eternal uphill struggle that I was facing, I forced myself to see it as motivational. As Hervé had said, with my accent, I would have to know significantly more about cheese than the customers to help them feel confident that I knew what I was talking about.

★ ★ ★

Work life in the shop was interesting. We were a small team and we worked a lot of hours in each other's company. In classic French style, egos were worn on sleeves and gossip passed at lightning speed. As I said, success required attention to detail and we were all guilty of forgetting things, which often led to heated debates. In many ways we were much like a family, and would fall in at very short notice to cover an illness or emergency. While there was the inevitable bickering that formed the background noise to any workplace, I was impressed at how focused everyone was in putting the shop ahead of themselves.

Every Thursday we would have a team meeting, where the trials and tribulations of the week were discussed, as were the challenges ahead. Mostly this revolved around making sure that there were enough of us present to cover any events such as cheese-and-wine evenings, or the busy Saturday morning rushes. I enjoyed these meetings a lot, and found that I was quickly able to contribute usefully. The eyes of a newcomer are useful for spotting problems that have been worked around for so long that they don't feel like problems any more.

It also turned out that my spreadsheet skills could be handy on occasion: before long I had consolidated the seven pages of our separate work schedules into one interactive multicoloured spreadsheet of joy. A massive boost to both morale and profitability, I'm sure!

This kind of behaviour seemed to have given me a reputation as a steady and reliable pair of hands. Perhaps it was deserved, I'm not sure, but necessity soon saw me taking on tasks that I really wouldn't have expected just weeks into my new position.

June, July and August are the holiday months in France (unsurprisingly) and these are flat times for the cheese trade. Consequently, each of the individual team members would take the majority of their annual leave over this period. That meant that I was coming into an understaffed shop and was almost immediately left on my own handling the shop for what could be rather extended tracts of time. I was taking restaurant orders, running till reconciliations and filling in the management accounting information. It was stressful at first, but really quite enjoyable.

It was almost incredible to realize that after less than a year in France I had managed to find a paid position in a French-speaking environment, a well-respected cheese shop with one of the Meilleurs Ouvriers de France, no less. On top of this unlikely turn of events, my opinion was now actually considered relevant and useful. Who would have thought it?

And, actually, it wasn't just the fact that I was working in the shop that was amazing: I was actually working in Les Halles de Lyon, a major destination on the gastronomic tourist trail. I remember serving a customer who had come from the US to a conference in Geneva. It was her first time in Europe and she had used her only free day to make the four-hour round trip to Lyon, just to visit Les Halles.

I was starting to build good relationships with the other traders, all at the top end of their respective industries — although that's not to say that there weren't a number of serious rivalries going on. When there is so much competition under one roof, it's only natural that there are some finely honed animosities. Everyone knew who shopped where and this resulted in a warmth and camaraderie between certain traders that was mirrored by a bitter chill and lowered gaze between others.

I got on well with a number of the shops surrounding us, particularly the butchers, whom we would regularly see in the underground levels of Les Halles, and who would generously give me a discount on the good cuts of meat whenever I fancied cooking a Sunday roast.

★　★　★

There were certainly regular customers to our shop and it was an absolute pleasure to help build up a relationship with them, anticipating their desires and, with feedback on their recent purchases, helping them to explore new cheeses. I have to confess that initially I spent a lot of time introducing our customers to two of my British favourites: Stilton and Stichelton. These sat very well among the French cheeses, and, before too long, I really didn't have to push all that hard: people were coming back for them of their own accord.

Of course, Les Halles had its fair share of big spenders, but some of the most interesting clients had more modest disposable income. There were a few clients like this who quickly became my favourites, such as the spectacularly tall and statuesque couple of students, who were eager to learn about cheese and would come every Wednesday during the quieter moments and spend time discussing what they had bought last time and what they would like to try this time — even if it was only a few small pieces. Often the guy would have a camera looped around his neck, and would take a few snaps of the displays as he waited to be served.

Another firm favourite of mine was Franck. Franck was retired, with an impressive paunch, a shuffling gait and a shock of bright, white hair. When we were quiet, he'd love to stand and chat to us, and he knew the whole team by name. Franck made no bones about the fact that he'd smoked his whole life, and his taste buds were only now paying the price. Every week, he would ask for the most potent cheese available. Anything less than tongue-burningly pungent would be considered bland and without interest. Sometimes, after my shift finished, I'd spot him sitting at the bar in the corner, sipping a frothy beer with a beatific smile on his wrinkled face.

A different type of clientele entirely were the mothers, who tended to come in waves just before the end of the school day. They would expertly peruse the display, looking for special offers and which cheeses were looking particularly good, before quickly trotting out a clear and concise order, invariably picking out our top cheeses of the moment with no need of guidance. What really blew me away was that, despite their appearance as connoisseurs, they regularly admitted that they didn't even like cheese, they were just buying it for their families.

★ ★ ★

The road to get here hadn't been easy, but I felt that I had done the right groundwork. I remember discussing it with Hervé; he told me, 'Matt, I'm employing you because you are ready for the job. You didn't look for short cuts: you started from the beginning and learned the correct way, through hard work.'

He had a good point. I think if I had started my cheese career in the shop it would have been really hard, if not disastrous. It would have taken a long time to get sufficiently up to speed to be able to serve effectively, and, worst of all, the doubters would have been right: I really would have given bad advice!

The path to Les Halles may not have been the smoothest, but I will be for ever glad that it was the one I took.

17

The Monger!

Alongside the cheese selling in Les Halles and the wholesale to restaurants and delicatessens, Etienne's shop also offered cheese-tasting evenings once a month or by reservation. These were guided tours through the intricacies of the cheese world, usually with a specific theme, such as cheeses from the north of France, goat's cheeses or blue cheeses. They were always highly generous in terms of quantity and quality, and particularly in respect of the wines that were involved in the pairings. I'm not sure whether Etienne ran a detailed budget for these events, but I doubt that he was making a huge amount of money.

That wasn't really the point though: the idea was to bring something a bit different, have some fun with our clients and to provide an interesting evening away from the standard (although undeniably excellent) restaurant fare that Lyon had to offer.

Within the first few weeks that I was working at the shop an event came up: a group of about fifteen senior staff members of a Lyon-based business looking for an evening of top-quality cheese and wine — the usual deal. Etienne had asked me if I minded being there to help out Guillaume in the presentation, and Séverine had offered to cover the food prep.

I was massively up for seeing how the whole arrangement worked and responded positively, looking forward to hearing how Guillaume would present the company and the cheeses and also getting a feel for the whole service side of the event, which I had absolutely no experience of. On the morning of the event, the organizer rang up and said that they had a number of English speakers with them and would prefer to have the evening in English. Etienne responded immediately with, 'Not a problem, I have an English guy on my team, he'll be happy to lead the event.'

Will he now? Cue cold sweat.

I didn't really have much choice and immediately got to work trying to learn as much as I could about the cheeses that had been selected. It's worth noting that at this point I had no experience whatsoever of acting as front-of-house, other than for house parties and dinner parties, and, frankly, I found even those quite trying. Even if you know how to lay a table, that doesn't help a huge amount when it comes to dressing a restaurant.

Still, the group, though difficult at times, were generally friendly and accepting of me and my 'pedigree' and I found to my delight that I could pretty satisfactorily answer their questions. Although I didn't necessarily enjoy the experience, having been thrust into it at such short notice, I felt that it was certainly something that I could handle in the future. The main thing was that, next time, I would want to have decided more or less what I was going to say significantly in advance.

★   ★   ★

It was at about this time that we met a couple in Lyon who ran a supper club, a sort of clandestine restaurant that on a roughly monthly basis threw a one-night, one-menu affair in a location not to be divulged until the night before. The model interested me a lot: it represented a relatively low-financial-risk approach to experimenting in both style and service. I knew of a couple of big success stories in the UK that had started this way.

Well, shortly into my time at the caves, our friends in Lyon had begun requesting tasters of the cheese that I was dealing with. Not surprising, really, as I talked about relatively little other than the enormous quantities of top-notch curd that I was handling on a regular basis.

Of course, we had friends over for dinner and always presented a generous cheese-board, and it was rare that I arrived at any social event without at least a little cheese in hand, or in pocket, or (on a bad day) in hair.

I wondered though if it would be possible to do something a bit more serious, a bit closer to the evenings that Etienne ran, but using the supper-club model. To be honest, I had no real interest in setting it up as a business in France, as the bureaucracy would have been outrageous for the tiny financial recompense. However, I thought that one day it might work well as a little earner in London that could be relatively easily slotted around other work commitments. It would also be a good way of keeping my hand in with up-to-date cheese knowledge, and also forcing my brain to think a bit more entrepreneurially.

That was for the future, though. What I wanted to do in Lyon would be a strictly-between-friends thing. I wouldn't make a profit but would just ask for contributions to cover my costs (like a mean dinner-party host — although our lucky guests would be receiving the benefit of my burgeoning cheese knowledge, so it wasn't all bad).

What I wanted to do was establish how the organization process worked — from the budgeting down to the cheese choices and style of presentation — and, hopefully, to iron out any wrinkles so that I could hit the ground running back in the UK. Critically, I also wanted to know if I enjoyed doing this kind of thing when it was me in charge. I had never really enjoyed giving presentations before, but I was buoyed up by the recent success at the shop. I guess it makes all the difference if you're passionate about what you're communicating.

* * *

I quickly got on to organizing my first evening. It would be based on a loose selection of my favourite cheeses and wines at that point in time, coupled with a few interesting aperitif ideas that I had picked up in the shop such as coupling dried fruits with fairly powerful washed-rind cheeses to create a rich balance of sweet and savoury. The important thing with this kind of balance was picking fruit that had a suitable length of finish compared with the cheese. It's a dangerous game introducing a potent cheese early on in the evening; some of the less cheese-hardy among your guests may need easing into the hardcore stuff.

The guest list was actually a group of American and Canadian ladies and their respective partners. Jen had met some of them at an expat female professional networking group and we had seen a fair number of them in Lyon bars and picnic spots when the weather allowed. They were invariably fanatical about food and making the most of what represented a limited stay in France.

They were a raucous bunch, full of questions, from the pertinent, about milk types and the step-by-step of how a cheese goes from fresh and young, to old and stinky, to the bizarre: Which cheeses float? Can you make cheese from whale milk?

I had huge fun chatting to them and sharing what I'd been learning, and it was clear that they respected the information that I was trying to convey. We had mentioned the fact that this might one day become a business and were met with a very enthusiastic response, which was heartening. Conversation then immediately turned to what such a business should be called, and the air was suddenly thick with cheese puns and ideas, from the ridiculous to the even more ridiculous.

Jen's friend Jen (who quickly came to be referred to as 'American Jen' to avoid confusion) and her partner Julien were very keen on the idea of some kind of portable cheese van. As this book goes to print, they will be newly married — congrats, guys!

'You could tap into all the cool, street-food-style stuff,' American Jen was saying, tucking a strand of blonde hair behind her ear and reaching for another slice of Comté, 'and you could pimp the van so it looked amazing.'

'Yeah,' chimed in Julien. 'You could have high-spec refrigeration, chrome surfaces, the works.'

'Hmm,' said Stacy, a softly spoken fellow foodie whose husband, Bjorn, had just bought her a three-week internship at the Paul Bocuse culinary institute for her thirtieth birthday — I almost exploded with envy when she told us about this! 'I like that idea, but what about going more retro? Almost like a cheese ice-cream truck.'

I couldn't help but grin at the identical looks of glee that settled on both my Jen's and American Jen's faces at this prospect. I have to say, this cheese-truck idea had never been on my agenda, but it was fun charting the cheesy possibilities.

'We still need a name though, for whatever

this business of yours might be,' pointed out Jen, starting to clear the table and giving my shoulder a squeeze on her way past.

'Matt!' shouted Jenna suddenly, from the other end of the table. 'I've got it!' Jenna was an articulate brunette from Canada. Intelligent and enthusiastic, she could usually be counted on for some interesting debate and well-reasoned arguments at dinner parties. Right now, though, she was bouncing excitedly in her seat, red wine threatening to slop over the edges of her glass.

'You should call yourself the Monger,' she said, clearly enjoying the word. 'It's clean, it's simple, it packs a punch.'

Jen and Stacy burst into giggles.

'Guys, I'm *serious*! Think about it: 'The Monger'.' This was said with such theatrical exuberance that even Jenna couldn't keep a straight face.

Although I appreciated the enthusiasm, I wasn't convinced by the name. The thought of an ice-cream-style van marauding through the streets of London with 'The Monger' emblazoned on it seemed slightly sinister. But I took their excitement to heart, and set about designing some business cards to hand out at future events.

★　★　★

239

The second event was a cheese-and-sparkling-wine evening, matching cheeses to a number of different wines and champagnes. The take-up on this was huge, and we ended up running a mini-event the week before so that everyone who was keen would get a taste.

The evening went very well, with the cheese-and-wine matches hugely enjoyed. It seems strange to think of sparkling wine as a cheese pairing but it's well worth a try, particularly if you can get your hands on a variety of wines with different levels of sweetness. One particular success well worth repeating was a fairly dry champagne with a mild double- or even triple-cream cheese, made with the addition of copious quantities of cream to give an intensely rich finish that is the perfect vehicle for complementary flavours such as truffle and ceps. The champagne cuts through the palate-coating texture, refreshing the taste buds and allowing secondary flavours to make themselves known.

My favourite pairing of the evening, however, was champagne with Parmesan. The Parmesan needs to be freshly cut and still slightly moist for this to work at its best. The champagne helps to highlight an effervescent quality in the Parmesan and really brings out the fruitiness of the mighty Italian cheese.

I felt that I was starting to hit my stride with these events. I had of course slightly mis-budgeted and not broken even, but that was OK. This was investment in our future.

★ ★ ★

It was just before Christmas and Lyon was starting to freeze again. I was getting pretty busy at the shop with prep for the Christmas rush and the competition (more on that later) and Jen had a lot on her plate. We were keen to have an event at our flat, though, a bit like a Christmas party but more cheese-driven, something that united a few of our disparate groups of friends in Lyon, notably the Americans and Canadians and the French friends we had met through Anne.

We made sure that the flat was well decorated, with a Christmas tree, fairy lights and candles, and took great pleasure in playing host.

The theme was winter cheeses, reflecting the seasonal nature of cheese and demonstrating a few different ways to enjoy it in the colder months. In retrospect, I was slightly overgenerous, serving individual *tartiflettes* and a baked Mont d'Or, otherwise known as Vacherin du Haut-Doubs, alongside a rather

241

generous selection of cheeses, all following on from piles of homemade Parmesan-and-paprika crisps. Jenna's wide-eyed look of fear at the size of the individual servings said it all!

The *tartiflette* recipe is a big favourite of mine, combining potato, onions, lardons, cream and lots of cheese. It's savoury and cheesy and doesn't skimp on flavour. It's the kind of food that you can reward yourself with after a day of skiing or when the weather is so cold that you just don't want to go outside. During our first winter in Lyon, the temperature didn't get above minus five Celsius for about two weeks, and often it was much colder, so much so that one of the rivers started to freeze over. I would have gone and looked if it hadn't been so bloody cold.

The recipe is considered by many to be a French family classic, but it's actually part of a rather successful marketing campaign created in the 1980s by the Syndicat Interprofessionnel du Reblochon as a means to sell more of the main cheesy ingredient, Reblochon, a round, flat, orange-rinded cow's-milk cheese from Savoie. For my personal take, I used an Abbaye de Tamié, a cheese made uniquely in the monastery bearing the same name also in the Savoie. It bears some resemblance to a Reblochon but with a much more spicy, full-bodied taste.

The Vacherin du Haut-Doubs, or 'Mont d'Or', is a brilliant cheese made on the French side of the mountainous border between Switzerland and France. There has been a significant amount of wrangling over whether the cheese was invented by the French or the Swiss, and who is allowed to call it what. The current position is that 'Vacherin du Haut-Doubs' and 'Mont d'Or' are the protected names for the French version and 'Vacherin Mont d'Or' is the name for the Swiss version.

If you've tried this cheese, you will know what the fighting was all about. It's awesome.

It comes in its own box in a wide variety of sizes and is aged in a ring of spruce bark, which imparts a subtle woody flavour. The cheese, when mature, is liquid and served with a spoon, but can easily be turned into a mini-fondue known as a *boîte chaude* (hot box) by placing it, lid on and wrapped in foil, in an oven until it's hot through and outrageously molten. It's fabulous when served with charcuterie and a Jura wine. When I introduced this to Jen's mum, she christened it 'magic spoon cheese' and the name has somewhat stuck in our house.

★　★　★

I had great fun with these events and am sure to carry on with them in London, but, in the meantime, I thought it might be nice here to include a little checklist of things that I learned that I really think could be applied to any cheese-and-wine evening that you might be planning:

1. Be careful what you promise in the invitation. If you say that you are going to provide four different wines, you do have to provide them, even if only two people can make it — at which point you're left with a hugely expensive wine cost per head, and probably a fairly vicious hangover the next morning.

2. Make sure you have enough cutlery and crockery. Sounds pretty obvious but check anyway. Equally, make sure you have enough chairs for everyone to sit down! We confidently stood back from the prep for our winter-cheeses evening, having been so chuffed at the number of people who had replied to our email advertising it. We were poised to welcome our guests, before suddenly clapping our hands to our foreheads and realizing that we had eight guests and only six chairs. Cue a mad scramble to the next-door neighbours for some chair begging.

3. Not everyone can eat as much cheese as you can. It's a sad fact, but you really do need

to take this into account. When you present the cheese, you don't want to see that look of fear on the guests' faces.

4. Enjoy it. Be part of the event, sit at the table and avoid pomposity at all costs — this can be hard when you're a massive cheese snob but it's vitally important.

18

Preparing for Battle

The first I had heard about the cheese competition known as the Concours National des Fromagers was in June 2012, shortly after arriving at the shop in Lyon. Séverine was giving me a rundown of the big events in the cheese calendar that really shouldn't be missed. She was telling me that one of the biggest would be the Salon International de la Restauration, de l'Hôtellerie et de l'Alimentation (or SIRHA), a large biennial restaurant-and-hospitality exhibition that would take place in January just outside Lyon. It was here that the prestigious Bocuse d'Or would be held, a huge international cooking competition that attracts some of the biggest names in the industry. Alongside the cheffing, there would also be a number of other highly regarded competitions in foodie fields such as *pâtisserie*, butchery and of course, cheese.

Being a curd nerd, I had come across such competitions before, mostly during late-night Internet searching, and had been consistently amazed at the way in which cheese could be worked to produce impressively towering platters of beautifully cut specimens in almost sculptural proportions.

It was while Séverine was talking about the magnificent cheese platters (and how Sabrina had previously competed and come third) that Etienne walked past.

'Don't you think Matt should enter the competition?' Séverine asked him, inexplicably and to my utter horror.

As the awkward silence filled the shop, the frown across Etienne's brow revealed his internal struggle to find a way of saying no without being too disheartening. In the end he chose not to express an opinion and walked off without saying anything. It was pretty clear that he didn't think it was a very good idea, but that didn't bother me in the least. I had been an employee for only a few weeks, after all. The inevitable humiliation that would ensue should I go up against people with serious experience frankly didn't appeal.

★ ★ ★

It wasn't until several months later that I heard mention of the competition again. I had been carrying on with my life and work, learning as much as I could and focusing on my sales pitch, but also trying hard to hone the manual skills that I'd been trained for in the caves, such as cutting and wrapping cheeses. These really weren't things that came naturally to me, and I wanted to prove that I had the dedication to improve. I was making progress, that much was clear, but I was far from perfect, and perfection was where I was aiming.

I was working in the shop one morning, wrapping cases of Saint-Marcellin, a small, potent and extremely runny cheese that's massively popular in Lyon. Actually, in terms of units sold, these are the shop's number one, and you'll find these cheeses on the menu of every Lyonnais restaurant. An important task for us is pre-wrapping the cheeses in branded cellophane to prevent them from running away during the day. Honestly, you can't leave them for a minute without their turning into creamy soup, which is less than ideal from a sales point of view, but is absolutely delicious when scooped up with a hunk of crusty bread.

Etienne sidled up to the opposite side of the central work surface, smiled, and slid across a piece of paper before heading back up to his office.

That piece of paper was the entrance form for the Concours National des Fromagers and the message was clear: I had his backing if I wanted to enter.

★ ★ ★

For me, choosing whether or not to take part in the competition was not easy. I had little objective measure of my ability outside the confines of the shop's immediate staff, and I also had no idea of the amount of time it would take to prepare and train. Would I endure four months of manic preparation only to come last — the embarrassing British failure?

In the end, having discussed it with Jen and Etienne, who were both very encouraging, I decided that it was worth the risk. It would be good to push myself and gain access to the higher level of training that would inevitably manifest when it was not just my reputation on the line, but also that of my employers. It was made very clear from the get-go, however, that in terms of my daily work I would receive next to no concession, and that any training would take place squarely within my own time.

With some significant trepidation, I posted my application.

The barrier to entry for the competition was apparently set relatively low. Simply 'be one of the first sixteen to apply.' However, applying when you weren't ready was not going to ingratiate you with the relatively small number of major players in the industry. These people, the aforementioned Meilleurs Ouvriers de France, take notice of such competitions and performing badly or, even worse, unprofessionally in front of them was unlikely to improve your career prospects, if it didn't annihilate them completely.

Additionally, a sensible applicant would certainly have a mentor to help with training for the event. Let's face it, if you couldn't find someone with the facilities, experience and wherewithal to train you, who believed that you had sufficient nous not to be an embarrassment to them, well, in that case, you hadn't really met the unspoken entry requirements.

★   ★   ★

I was not the only member of our shop staff to enter. Victor had also filled in the form. He, too, had the backing of Etienne and we were both very motivated to train together. We made a pact that we would support each other right up to the instant that the competition began, at which point it would be each man for himself.

The names of the successful applicants would not be revealed for several weeks, but we started training immediately. The application form contained details of the different challenges and we got to work finding ways to incorporate the necessary skills into our daily lives.

The main challenge revolved around presenting a platter of twenty-five different cheeses, ten of which would be selected at random from the French AOP cheeses and the rest by the competitors. On the day, three of the ten preselected cheeses would be picked out of a hat and would be tasted by the jury, while the candidates wrote out technical information sheets relating to the histories and regulations around production of the cheeses, as well as tasting notes and sensible serving suggestions.

Other than practising neat cuts and quizzing each other on obscure cheese facts, there was little that could be done in terms of preparation here, although we both did a lot of review of what had gone on in previous competitions.

Where we *could* make an early start, however, was with the other challenges, particularly in cutting cheese to precise weights without scales, and wrapping cheeses perfectly. This was the day job and I made it a habit to estimate in my head the weight of every slice cut. I would also regularly tour the shop and try to guess the weights of cheeses, either cut or whole, before weighing them to see if I was right.

This is surprisingly difficult, as cheeses have very different densities depending on how they have been made, but I developed a method that more or less worked. I would, for each family of cheese, hone a mental image of a rectangular slice that weighed 100 grams, and, for the largest wheels, the arc of rind required to create a 1-kilo point. I would then use basic mental geometry to scale up (or down) to any weight that I required, taking into account the length of the slice and the depth of the cheese.

Did I always get it right?

Absolutely not, but at least it was a logical starting point to build from.

Wrapping cheese is an interesting one. In some shops, there is a prescribed style of wrapping, and there are publications that purport to detail the 'correct' way to wrap certain types of cheese. However, there are many ways to achieve a neat wrap and in our shop we were left entirely to our own creative devices. I kept my eye on the work of others, copying where I liked what I saw, and honing what I already knew. There is something bizarrely satisfying about wrapping a cheese well, and never let it be said that this isn't a transferable skill — I am now responsible for wrapping all of the Christmas presents! Sometimes I think Jen buys particularly weirdly shaped ones just to test me. With cheese, there are a number of considerations to take into account, notably good coverage of any cut surfaces, neatness, a wrap that doesn't undo of its own accord and also sufficient paper that, once the cheese has been nibbled at by the client, they can then wrap it back up again. If you have to resort to tape, you're doing it wrong.

Then there was the blind tasting, which we practised near constantly. Eating copious amounts of cheese in the name of training could hardly be described as a hardship, after all. I would regularly have just finished serving a customer when Victor, having snuck up behind me (usually when I was carrying something and couldn't resist), would push an unknown lump of cheese into my mouth and ask me what it was as I was struggling for air. Happy times!

We would comment incessantly on each other's style and performance, questioning each other on the contents of the rules and regulations surrounding the AOP cheeses and picking holes in each other's sales patter. It was massively motivating and it changed the energy of the shop.

Before the announcement of the candidates was made, we started to receive some initial emails from the competition organizers, providing the complete set of rules and the list of cheeses that we would be required to source. These emails had been copied rather than blind-copied, so we had a fair idea of who had applied (cue copious Internet research), but it appeared that the list of recipients was in chronological order of application. If that assumption held, it looked very much as if Victor and I would make the cut.

It was at this point, however, that things started to get a bit shady. The competition was organized by the Syndicat des Crémiers-Fromagers Rhône-Alpes/PACA, a regional union of cheese sellers. Etienne, being a notable cheese seller in the region, had strong connections with the Syndicat. He told me with a smirk that during a conversation with the organizers they wanted to know if one of the entrants from his shop was indeed English, and what on earth it would mean if an *Englishman* should win the competition. Etienne had apparently stood up for me and pointed out that the rules made no mention of nationality and simply stated that applicants had to be working in the industry.

I wasn't quite sure what to make of this information, but at the time it did feel as though my nationality might make things at the competition harder. Would the prejudices against the English and their understanding, or perceived lack of it, about cheese really come in to play here? To be honest, I was worried that I might be in trouble, particularly given some of the attitudes that I had come across with our more traditionally minded Lyonnais customers.

Shortly afterwards, another call was made to Etienne from the organizers. The application deadline had passed and the applicants had been counted. This year, there had been substantially more interest than expected, in part boosted by a number of cases where multiple entrants were representing one shop — Victor and I being a prime example.

The organizers wanted to massage the applications to be more nationally representative (apparently, a large proportion of the first sixteen to apply hailed from Lyon) and to show a wider selection of shops. Consequently, a new rule had been introduced to allow only one entrant per business. It was to be me or Victor.

This was a massive blow. We both wanted it

badly, and had both already committed a fair amount of time to the preparation. For my part, I was well aware that I would get only one shot at a competition like this, my time in France was limited, and I was already over halfway through my agreed career break. Victor was planning to be in Lyon for longer than I was but that didn't make it feel any fairer.

An emergency meeting was held by Etienne, Victor and me where it was decided that, unable to change the thoroughly unpleasant situation, the decision would go down simply to the one of us who had been in the shop the longer. That was me, but not by much.

Victor was not happy, and neither was I, but the decision had to be made and there it was. Now I had even more to prove.

★　★　★

It was clear to all that I was an underdog, but Etienne pointed out that, in this industry, underdogs could make it big. He used himself as a case in point.

Etienne had grown up in the Drôme, a department in the Rhône-Alpes renowned for its goat's cheeses. He told me that as a child he had 'bathed in milk' — a reference to the fact that his grandparents were cheese makers. In later life he found himself in the restaurant business, notably on the service side, and eventually he began providing training in the much-acclaimed Institut Paul Bocuse and its restaurant. Among other responsibilities, he took care of the selection and presentation of cheeses.

The Concours National des Fromagers was launched in 1997, and has been a great way of promoting the industry, as the photogenic platters slip easily into the visual media. However, the competition has also served as something of a training ground for the more rigorous Meilleurs Ouvriers de France competition. The first of these competitions took place in 2000 and included a certain Hervé Mons among its number. In fact, just about everyone in the select group of cheese MOFs has taken part in the Concours National des Fromagers at some point.

Invitations were sent out widely, not just to cheese sellers, but to everyone working in the industry, and so it was that a young Etienne Boissy entered the competition, not expecting great success but willing to give it his best. He was placed third and, off the back of this, took the highly unusual step of entering the running for the 2004 MOF cheese competition, where, against all odds, he succeeded.

Unusual? Against all odds, how so?

The rules of the MOF categories, including such diverse ones as cooking, cauldron making and cheese selling, state the requirement for several years' experience. However, they don't require that these years be in the relevant discipline, it's just assumed that this will be the case. The fact that Etienne did not own a cheese shop, nor did he work directly in the cheese industry, made it look very unlikely that he would be able to perform at a sufficient level to attain the blue, white and red collar.

It is thus with justifiable pride that he wears his MOF collar at Les Halles today.

* * *

With the Christmas rush finally over, the shop, the caves and Les Halles in general let out a near-audible sigh of relief. But for some of us it wasn't time to relax just yet: it meant full steam ahead for competition preparation.

Actually, Jen and I did manage some snatched respite over Christmas, sufficient for me to propose, and for her to agree to marry me!

* * *

On top of my personal training in the shop, Hervé had also arranged courses for me and two others from the Mons family who were also entering the competition: Loan, a young and enthusiastic guy whom I'd met while working at the caves, and Geraldine, whom I'd come across briefly in the Montbrison shop. The first of these group training sessions was a cheese-carving course with William Hermer, the 2012 French Champion of fruit and vegetable sculpture (I would recommend a quick Internet search here, as his work is beyond spectacular). Through the decimation of vast quantities of soap, which is slightly easier to work with than cheese and much less expensive, we learned some basic techniques in carving.

I was taken by the possibilities of carving cheese and spent much time practising on some of the harder cheeses, and anything else I could get my hands on. Jen would frequently pick up an apple to take a bite, only to find that half of it had been carved into a rose, or a crude approximation of a tractor or a dinosaur. The problem was that it was time-consuming and, with one slip, you could not only lose all of your hard work, but also a finger. Difficult and potentially dangerous work under a very tight time restriction? Sounded like fun to me. I figured that very few others would attempt a cheese sculpture, so it might be a good way to set myself apart with a novel technique. I just needed to pick one shape and practise it often until it was second nature.

The main boost to my training, however, was François Robin, a MOF who had qualified in the class of 2011 under the tutelage of Hervé. François was rarely seen without a smile and was very personable, but when he got down to it, and things got serious, he was exceptionally professional. His in-depth knowledge of the rules of the competition was impressive. This was coupled with a very quick understanding and insight into our characters (and potential flaws), and a calm and fluid technique when working with the cheeses.

He read easily between the lines of the communications that we had received from the organizers and showed us how to do the same. The organizers didn't always speak directly through their guidance, but, when you looked for it, their hints were clear. Reading between the lines, I inferred the following:

- the cheese is king — don't mutilate it for the sake of aesthetics;
- there are lots of marks for demonstrating a theme;

- don't hide the cheese with unnecessary decoration;
- don't bring lots of fiddly supports for the cheese.

We had two days with François in January prior to the competition. During the first he did spectacularly well at inspiring 'the fear'. I realized that, with three weeks to go, I had a truly enormous amount of work to do to get myself up to speed.

While never saying as much, François led me to the painful and highly unwelcome realization that my ideas to this point were derivative and poorly executed. It was time to go back to the drawing board for my presentation piece.

He helped me see that cheese presentations, like most things in life, are subject to ever-evolving fashions. Having being made MOF in the most recent round, he had his finger on the pulse. Ferns, grapes and straw were firmly out. His suggestions for the competition, while not exactly minimalist, certainly didn't shy away from cold, blockish and linear cuts — rustic was dead and buried.

The nature of this moving fashion was best highlighted through the vastly different aesthetic judgements and technical considerations provided by Hervé, Etienne and

François, who had attained their MOF collars in 2000, 2004 and 2011 respectively. Being pulled in three different directions, I chose to take my picks from each but ultimately to chart my own path.

I decided on a crescent-moon theme for my platter. This was for a number of reasons but, significantly, it was a visual cue that required no verbal explanation. Additionally, the shape bore much similarity to traditional (i.e. circular) cheese shapes, meaning that the link to the original form would never be too distant in anyone's mind.

Alongside this training, I was doing my best to source good-quality cheeses for the big day. We Mons candidates were at an advantage here compared with some of the others, as we had access to the caves with their huge diversity of cheese at varying stages of *affinage*, and Hervé's links to international *affineurs* and exporters. That said, proper preparation prevents piss-poor performance, so I started early, quickly choosing which cheeses I would source directly from the caves and which would come from elsewhere. I made the contacts and ensured that the cheeses would arrive in plenty of time for me to check that they were OK and to add my personalized touch to the *affinage*.

It was a difficult call choosing the

affinages: a good cheese platter should take into account the environment that it will find itself in and this one would be harsh. The competition space would be hot and dry and the platters would be left for a long period of time. The choice of a runny cheese would have been a presentational catastrophe: it would have escaped the building by the time that the results were announced!

Fancy a rundown of my cheese choices?

First off, we had the cheeses that were required by the judges. These were all selected from the French AOP cheeses and therefore included some very familiar faces and firm favourites.

There was good old dependable Roquefort, the piquant and classic ewe's-milk blue cheese, and Salers, the mighty and uncompromising cow's-milk cheese from Auvergne. I was pleased to see Fourme de Montbrison on the list, and would be very happy to show a cheese from the Plagne farm on my platter. Another two pleasant surprises were Langres, that washed-rind cow's-milk cheese with mild creamy heart that I had enjoyed working with in the caves; and Abondance, an all-too-often overlooked, cooked, cow's-milk Alpine cheese with its buttery, nutty taste and bitter, spicy finish.

These formed a solid starting point,

around which I was able to place the cheeses that I felt should be there, that represented my tastes and personal cheesy tendencies. My goal was to be inclusive of as many styles of cheese, different milks and different countries of origin as I could, while bearing in mind that the quality had to be top-notch.

The first step, of course, was finding some stunning British cheese, so, with the help of Neal's Yard Dairy, I found a fine West Country Farmhouse Cheddar — a raw-milk, farm-produced version of the generally insipid, yellow plastic found in the supermarkets. This was the real deal with its rich, complex, savoury flavour and yellow crumbling pâte. I also chose a Stilton, the king of cheeses as far as I'm concerned, with its divine buttery pâte and sophisticated blue tang, which would complement the Roquefort nicely.

For a bit of height and volume, I called upon a distinguished Suisse Gruyère and a badass Beaufort Chalet d'Alpage, two of my favourite cheeses at the shop, which had a habit of finding their way into my shopping basket.

With a nod to the Italians, I selected a fine Taleggio, a punchy (when aged) cow's-milk cheese with an orange rind and sackloads of character. This cheese was regularly eaten for lunch *chez nous*, grilled on an artisanal baguette, hot, gooey and full of flavour. I was also keen to present a Parmigiano-Reggiano, mostly because I felt that it merits a place on a cheese board, rather than being relegated to powdering the family bolognese.

Given that Vacherin du Haut-Doubs, that gooey favourite, was in full season at the time of the competition, I was of course keen to get it on the platter. The spruce-bark band would help to keep the cheese from running away under the heat of the lights.

Goat's-milk cheeses were pretty well represented in the required-cheeses selection, but ewe's-milk cheeses noticeably less so. For a change of colour and style, I chose Piacentinu Ennese, a Sicilian Pecorino-style cheese made with a strong infusion of saffron and peppercorns in the milk. It had massive flavour and a bright sunshine-yellow colour that really popped on the platter. I also served up a Corsican Brocciu, a mild, fresh cheese that can be made either with goat's or ewe's milk (mine was the latter). I served this with a tasty cherry jam, a brilliant pairing.

* * *

In the two weeks leading up to the competition I was preparing frantically, working at the shop in the mornings and then staying through the afternoons to practise preparing my platter within the time allowance and my best representation of the conditions of the competition. In the evenings I was up late swotting up on the ten cheeses that I might be tested on and putting finishing touches to the all-important descriptive labels for my cheeses that would be displayed on the platter. These would have a big impact on the overall look of the presentation piece, and I was experimenting with colours, shapes and sizes, and laminating everything like a man possessed. At one stage I thought about getting extra-creative, and had poor Jen writing haiku in French about each of the cheeses on my platter. She did a sterling job, but in the end I decided it was just too much, and stuck to something more minimalist. With hindsight, I realize this was definitely a wise decision. Expert cheese judges and poetry are not known to be a particularly harmonious mix.

19

Competition Time

I was stressed. It was only to be expected, really. I've never gone into an exam in my life feeling calm, and this was no different. Actually, in some ways it was worse: traditionally, and certainly when you sit a tax or organic-chemistry exam, there isn't a crowd watching you and big video cameras all up in your business.

There were just too many variables that I didn't feel on top of: I would be transporting the cheeses in the shop's van, which I had never driven before; I had no idea how long it would take to get to the exhibition centre, and I was pretty sure that significant elements of the information that I had tried to cram into my brain the night before had fallen out while I was asleep — or, rather, as I turned restlessly and prevented Jen from sleeping. I avoided mentally prodding the ball of information in my head, just in case more of it turned out to have disappeared, or decided to fall out of my ears en route.

On the morning of 27 January, Jen and I

found our way to Les Halles, where we were wished good luck by the butchers (who were of course already at work — in all my time at Les Halles, I had never once seen them arrive). We made our way to the van with my teetering piles of crates. We were on time and all was marginally less stressful.

I sat in the driver's seat, adjusting the height and mirrors and noting that there was no rear-view. All was good, engine on, and then — Hang on a minute! Where's the handbrake? It quite simply was nowhere to be found. Panic started to set in: do the French even *have* handbrakes? Where do they keep them? Why is this happening to me?

Five minutes later I was pulling away from the parking space in a nervous sweat. The roads at that time in the morning were calm, which was a plus, as I didn't have quite as much control over the van as I would have liked. The only way that I had found to apply the handbrake was to deliberately stall, and then, afterwards, taking it off again was hit or miss. Unfortunately, Lyon is full of traffic lights. Every time I sped up or slowed down, the crates of oh-so-important and fragile cheese slid from the front of the van to the back with a loud and cringe-making thud.

We arrived, parked loudly and embarrassingly, and clipped a barrier as we did so.

Loan and Geraldine were there with their supporters, Cédric from the Montbrison shop and Aurélie and Romain from the caves. Coffee was consumed, nervous chatter was exchanged.

There were sixteen competitors, split into two groups by a small child with a hat full of names. As there was only enough space for eight to compete at once, the remaining eight were to be locked up in a room and forced to wait impatiently for their chance to shine.

I was immediately relieved to be in the first wave. Just think, I told myself. In two hours it will all be over and you can resume a normal life!

The competition was set up in such a way that each competitor was enclosed in one of eight identical, sterile kitchens, about 5 metres squared with ovens, sinks and a sea of stainless-steel work surfaces. They were almost boxes really, with high partitions to stop us from being able to see what the others were doing. The front of the box was open and faced out into a crowd of spectators.

The staging was starting to fill up and as I looked out at the crowd I could see a number of friendly faces. I took a lot of deep breaths, did a frankly obsessive amount of wiping down and organizing my materials and then . . .

Oh shit!

I'd forgotten to bring a cutting board! How was I going to cut my cheese? I frantically gestured to Jen, who came running over. She asked Cédric what could be done and he said he'd ask around but to try not to worry: he'd won the competition before without a cutting board. Funnily enough, his words did little to ease my sweating palms. Thankfully, Geraldine wasn't competing until the second half of the competition, and she very kindly let me use hers. In a slightly demented and adrenaline-fuelled sign language, I gestured that I would buy her a drink later, and hoped the cameras weren't filming my flailing too much.

And then we were off. The master of ceremonies, a well-known cheese MOF named Bernard Mure-Ravaud — with some of the most impressive facial hair I have ever seen — started the clock. I searched out Jen's face in the crowd. She gave me a wink and started clapping, and then I tried my hardest to tune out the cameras and the noise from the crowd and everything else. I needed to focus if I wanted this to be anything other than a disaster.

First up were the three cheeses chosen by the judges for tasting. They had randomly selected the Langres, the Neufchâtel and

Tome des Bauges. I was very happy with the examples of these that I'd chosen. I was confident that they were good representations of the cheese and that I was able to do them justice in explaining my choice of *affinage*.

I had been carefully washing my batch of Langres for the last week and a half, and had selected the best of the bunch, somewhere between orange and golden in colour. I knew that, inside, the pâte was almost exactly half creamy and half whitely solid and slightly acidic in the centre, the perfect interplay of fruity sweetness and palate-cleansing acidity while marrying two very different textures.

The Neufchâtel was also a young example chosen again for that interplay of textures with a small creamy layer. It also helps to push to the forefront the unexpected texture that comes from the slow, predominantly lactic-acid-based coagulation used in its manufacture.

There was a slight question mark hanging over my Tome des Bauges, which was perhaps a little further gone than I would have liked. The one that I had tasted from the same batch the night before had had a rather aggressive bite at the tail-end of its finish, but the texture was great.

I explained my cheeses as well as I could, trying not to stumble over any of the vocab, even though my tongue felt furred by nerves. The judges seemed receptive to what I was saying, and, as I wrote down the technical details of each of the cheeses, I was by no means confident, but I was certainly feeling as if I had at least put in a credible effort. So far, so not catastrophic.

Then it was time for the big event: the cheese platter. Forty-five minutes to show the world that I deserved to be here.

As the start was announced, my hands were shaking and my brow sweating. It was hot, my tie was constricting and the presence of the cameras was unbelievably offputting. I was reluctant to make my cuts under that much attention. François's suggestion that we start with the easy bits first seemed like really good advice; what a shame that I hadn't followed it!

I focused on the stopwatch and the cheeses in hand, taking a moment every now and then to take some calming deep breaths and to search out the encouragement emanating from Jen and my friends in the crowd. As the countdown dwindled away, I could see my planned structure taking shape. I had designed the platter to be roughly symmetrical, with points of colour generally mirrored horizontally. The most striking feature was the tall, vertically presented point of Suisse

Gruyère, which had been aged for almost two years and was a rich yellow, studded with the amino-acid crystals that tend to build up over time. I had removed a circle from the point and suspended a disc of Fourme de Montbrison within it; the faint blue marbling running through the pale cheese was reminiscent of a lunar landscape.

In front of the Gruyère was perhaps my favourite part of the platter: the Fourme de Montbrison. Using a combination of angled and straight cuts, I was able to mount a near-perfect circle of the centre of the cheese vertically, sitting on a vertically cut base, to give the illusion that the two were one piece. By removing an off-centred circle from the disc (part of which went into the Gruyère), I was able to create a large and elegant moon shape.

These two cheeses were effectively the backbone of the display, and were supported by diagonally mounted wings of a stunning Beaufort Chalet d'Alpage and a slice of well-aged Parmesan, a rather unusual presentation. I included two spires of cheese, the Montgomery Cheddar and the Salers, cut with a butter wire that was designed to leave elegant curved indents. There were a number of other complicated cuts, mostly on a bias, and a few more fiddly elements such as the crescent-moon carving in the Mimolette and the intricate slicing and rotating of the Valençay to form one stepped pyramid, which rose up in a spiral, each section of the pyramid showing off just a hint of the cheese's delicate white flesh. Some of these elements were deliberately slightly hidden from immediate view on the platter. I wanted people to be able to spot something new each time they looked at it.

I was aware that I perhaps wasn't going to achieve everything that I had hoped, but it would meet the requirements of the competition and have enough cheeses on the platter. I thought that I had probably shown a reasonable bit of technical achievement and a degree of whimsy, and I had to admit: the cheeses looked pretty good.

Time seemed to be going at lightning speed, and, almost before I knew it, Bernard was leading the crowd in the final ten-second countdown. When the time was up, each of the platters was carried from its respective box to a separate room for judging. I was in the penultimate box in the row, and so was able to catch little glimpses of my competitors' pieces as they trundled past. My platter suddenly felt very minimalist. I saw several with floral decoration, one that appeared to have been covered in sand and featured a lighthouse in the centre of it, and one very dramatic piece featuring a Langres on a motorized turntable, lots of trailing ivy, and dry ice bubbling out of theatrical goblets. My moon theme really was very basic compared with all of this, and I only hoped the judges would appreciate my focus on the cheeses, rather than bemoaning the lack of decoration.

There was no time to fret, though, as I was immediately presented with the next challenge: a mountain of cheese to cut to weight and wrap neatly without a set of scales. This was the day job and I had been practising for months — but that didn't make it any easier. I knew that this was largely a game of chance as variability in the thickness and density of a given cheese is very difficult to judge. I focused on neat cuts and a utilitarian wrapping style.

I had been remarkably nervous about the paper that we would use to wrap with as it was a complete unknown. It may sound odd — OK, it *does* sound odd — but one of the most disturbing things to happen at work in the run-up to Christmas was a change in our supplier of cheese paper. The thickness had changed slightly, as had the coefficient of friction. Bearing in mind that by this point I had wrapped tens of thousands of pieces of cheese and that muscle memory had long ago taken over, the impact of really very minor changes in flexibility and friction of the paper was shocking. Perhaps like suddenly finding that your keyboard required twice as much pressure to register a letter being typed. It didn't quite fold right, or slide right, and, where I had usually prided myself on neatness, I found myself looking scruffy and cack-handed.

I needn't have worried, though: the paper in the competition was a dream to use, light, airy and responsive. Although I couldn't speak for how well it protected the cheese, it definitely handled better than the paper at our shop. I lined up my wrapped cheeses like little presents for the judges, and waited for the next and final part of the test: the blind tasting.

I was presented with a selection of three unknown cheeses for which I had to deduce the name, the origin, the type of milk, the method of production and the age. As I opened the small, white cardboard box I suppressed a smile. I recognized two immediately by sight. There was a Pont-l'Évêque from Normandy and the slightly less well-known Bleu du Vercors-Sassenage from the Rhône-Alpes. The third was one of three possibilities, which I would have to rely on my palate to narrow down. It was definitely one of the large, pressed, uncooked cheeses: Cantal, Laguiole or Salers. Salers was pretty easy to eliminate due to its massive and uncompromising farmyard tang, which this mystery cheese lacked. The differences between Laguiole and Cantal can be difficult. The piece in front of me had the milky edge that often reminds me of a young Cheddar. To my palate, Laguiole tends towards a more buttery texture and bitter finish, leading me to the conclusion that the cheese I was sampling was in fact a Cantal.

I scribbled down my answers and, checking my stopwatch, realized that there were still five minutes on the clock. The quality of the samples was great, and it was a pleasure to eat them, although I felt that restraint was probably wise, taking just enough to ensure that my analysis was correct.

And then suddenly, it was all over — time to wipe down, again, and let the next eight competitors do their thing. As I left the box, I wished luck to the next incumbent, who was waiting in the wings, gave Geraldine back her cutting board and returned my cheeses to the van, feeling immediately several stone lighter and massively drained.

Geraldine and Loan were both in the second eight and I was keen to see how they would get on, and get a good look at the rest of my competition. Everyone was looking on top form and some of the ideas were great. It was a pleasure to watch the level of seriousness and professionalism on display, despite the fact that it probably meant that a good position for me was becoming more and more unlikely.

It was confirmed: almost everyone except for me had put at least some form of decoration on their platter. Damn! I clung to the hope that my platter would stand out more because of this, but I couldn't help thinking that the judges would view the lack of decoration as a big, fat black mark against my name.

The second eight finished up just before midday, and the results weren't due to be announced until five in the afternoon. The wait for the results was interminable. Normally the food-oriented exhibition would have been fascinating but I just didn't care. I was reeling from a brutal adrenaline crash and running pretty much on empty. All I wanted was a sleep, but that clearly wasn't going to happen, there didn't even seem to be any chairs and the immense interlocking halls and unending stands all pushing their latest and greatest wares felt suffocating — not helped by the furnace-like temperature that we were subjected to.

Jen and I wandered through the labyrinthine exhibition centre, tasting small nibbles here and there and desperately trying to find somewhere to sit down. We ended up back at the competition stage, where the butchers were battling it out. I was happy to let myself be almost hypnotized by the trussing, stuffing and mincing of the six duos who were competing.

★   ★   ★

Five *loooooooooong* hours later Jen and I were carrying my cheese platter to the special area set aside for the prizegiving. A number of stands had been set up to receive the displays, although by that point a large crowd had gathered, so manoeuvring the incredibly delicate (and quite heavy) platter was a somewhat tricky operation.

The MOFs were out in force: I counted more than ten of them, perhaps fourteen, although the way that they were shifting around made fixing down the numbers rather difficult. I recognized a large number of them. These were the real big cheeses of France and it made me feel pretty star-struck to see them in the flesh.

Etienne had arrived, as had Séverine, and they were busy grilling me on how it had all gone. Etienne remained stony-faced when looking at my platter. I tried to read his expression to see what he thought of my work, but there was nothing forthcoming.

I caught a few murmurs from the crowd that there was a lot of empty space on mine. It was clear that I was sparse in comparison with everyone else. Someone across the room from me had even carved a boat out of their cheese, with three little discs of goat's cheese resting inside, and a sail made of waxed cheese paper.

I resigned myself to an OK, if not exceptional, performance, but then who knew how badly I'd done in the rest of the competition? Perhaps, if the rest had gone well, I might still have come third. I'd entered this thing as a challenge, to stretch myself and to see whether or not I could even dream of being considered on a level with French cheesemongers. All I wanted was not to come last, but, as the announcer started warming up the crowd, I couldn't help but start eyeing the podium with envy.

Finally, it was time for the results. The MOFs, in their white uniforms with red, white and blue collars, lined up behind the stage and their joking and horseplay quietened down. I noticed that Hervé had joined the group.

I was standing in the crowd with Jen, waiting to be able to shake hands with the winner and leave gracefully before getting an early night. There was a lot of talking, a lot of thanking the sponsors and a lot of handshaking going on on stage. And then, all of a sudden, the prizes were being announced. Third place went to the youngest competitor, a pretty girl named Myriam. I couldn't help but smile at the expression on her face. She looked absolutely flabbergasted to be called up to the stage. Second place also went to a female competitor — Laëtitia — whose platter had high, structured peaks at the back, and intricate cuts of cheese down at the front, decorated liberally with purple flowers. I had remembered seeing this one come past me while I was in my box earlier, and thinking it looked feminine, but very impressive.

Then there was more beating about the bush from the judges. They were trying to build the anticipation before announcing the coveted first prize, but my mind was starting to drift.

'And the winner . . . '

I'm really looking forward to relaxing. All this forced smiling is making my face sore. Still, just in case I'm in any of the photos . . .

' . . . by a clear margin, and with a unanimous vote . . . '

I'm quite hungry, actually. I wonder what's in the fridge. Did I remember to get anything in for tonight?

'. . . is Mathieu . . . '

I didn't realize there was another Mathieu in the competition.

'. . . Feroze!'

Bloody hell!

20

Celebration and Celebrity

I stood there, paralysed, before turning to Jen, who was jumping up and down and cheering with a huge smile on her face. I looked across the crowd, where Victor and Séverine had climbed onto chairs and were whooping and punching the air. Time stopped for a short instant in which my brain just about managed to register that they really were talking about me. Then the crowd parted and I was pushed up onto the stage. I was handed a trophy and a certificate, and then more gifts and prizes in bags were piled into my arms as I struggled to perform my best smile in front of the camera flashes, and not to drop anything on the floor.

Hervé and Etienne were already behind me on the stage and hugged and kissed me on the cheek in a kind of French, masculine, congratulatory way. The next thing I knew I was being interviewed by a presenter with a camera from one of the major French TV stations. In the shock of the moment, my brain hadn't quite engaged and I stumbled slightly. The presenter asked, 'Does he even speak French?' Hervé leaped to the microphone and said some very complimentary things, which unfortunately were all cut from the TV programme. The fact that my stammering was cut, too, can only be seen as a blessing.

The wall of cameras eventually receded and I was able to leave the stage and talk to Jen, Etienne and my other colleagues from the shop.

'You did it, bro!' Victor shouted, giving me a hug.

As we were trying to make sense of what had happened, a massive sense of relief descended with the knowledge that the slog was over and now I would be able to relax a little. Christmas (as always in the cheese world) had been a mad dash, and, due to the competition, life hadn't slowed down since. I was looking forward to spending some quality time with Jen, properly celebrating our engagement, and getting the chance to see my friends. It still hadn't sunk in. I kept replaying the announcement in my head, and each time I felt just as stunned.

I took a few minutes out of the *mêlée* to ring my parents and tell them the good news. They were just as shocked as I was, but very happy for me. The milling crowds hadn't dispersed (I think they were waiting for the official OK to fall upon the cheese platters and demolish them) and people kept coming up to me to shake my hand, offer congratulations and sometimes even pose for pictures with me, which I found truly bizarre! I enjoyed watching people attack my platter; having seen the journey that each of those carefully picked morsels went through to get there, to have thrown them away at the end would have been criminal!

I was approached by a number of the MOFs, who congratulated me on my achievement. I had been following this elite group in the media for a long time now, and it seemed insane that they were now approaching me to offer their thoughts and wish me well for the future. I was touched by how welcoming and friendly the majority of them were. That said, a few ignored me completely and one well-known name in the business made a point of walking past me and Etienne, commenting loudly and deliberately in our earshot, to no one in particular, that he was 'frankly disturbed that the Champion de France had been awarded to an Englishman'.

Well, you can't please everyone.

★   ★   ★

Elation gave way to fatigue as the lack of sleep caught up with me. It felt as if I had spoken to everyone that I needed to: I'd thanked the organizers, those who had trained me and everyone who had come out to support me. Unfortunately, however, there was still work to do. I needed to return the unused cheese to the shop so that it could be sold. The platter was given up as free game but there were some serious bits of cheese in the van that needed to go back to Les Halles.

The journey here in the van had been bad enough, but the thought of tackling it now, while running on so much adrenaline, was not an appealing prospect! Thankfully, Victor and his wife came to the rescue, and offered to drive me, Jen and the van full of cheese back to the shop, where we would be able to unload everything.

★ ★ ★

By the time we had finally returned home, it was getting on for 9 p.m., and I was struggling to stay awake. Jen had made sure that all the ingredients were in for one of my favourite recipes, a dry and spicy lamb curry. We were both covered in cheese, and feeling rather shell-shocked. Jen started chopping onions and garlic, and I slumped down on the sofa. We just couldn't wipe the smiles off our faces. I won. I *won*!

My phone rang. It was Etienne.

'Matt, you and Jen aren't busy this evening, are you?' he asked.

'Well, we're — '

'Great, we'll be over to pick you up in fifteen minutes. We've got an invite to l'Abbaye de Collonges. Dress smart!'

Having lived in Lyon for over a year, we knew that the Abbaye was one of the jewels in the crown of the Paul Bocuse Empire, not his thrice-Michelin-starred restaurant, but his ornate banqueting hall. We didn't need to be asked twice. The curry was abandoned and we frantically changed and groomed ourselves to look less frazzled and cheese-encrusted, and more ready for a once-in-a-lifetime dining experience. Turning up to one of the finest dining establishments in the world with bits of Gruyère stuck to your face is probably frowned upon, after all.

★   ★   ★

We arrived late, and had missed the champagne reception, but it was hard to be too devastated given the magnitude of the sumptuous surroundings, and we happily filed into the dining room.

The sight that greeted us was one of the most fantastic and bizarre I think I have ever seen. We entered the dining room of this temple to refined and elegant haute cuisine to music. Chopin, you might be thinking, or maybe Debussy. Wrong. Traditional fairground music was blasting out of an enormous, and enormously elaborate, fairground pipe organ, which stood proudly at the far end of the room. It was massive! It took up the entire far wall, and was painted in candy colours. There were small, mechanized figures that would trumpet and drum with panache, and there was even a small version of the famous Mr Bocuse himself, merrily conducting away with a wooden spoon as his baton. It was incredible, in the literal sense of the word, but completely wonderful at the same time, and I noticed that all the other diners had the same look of dazed but childlike glee on their faces as they found their tables and sat down.

The meal was exquisite, down to every last detail. The food was, as you'd expect, delicious and the service staff were attentive and incredibly athletic. For the service of desserts, with more raucous fanfare in the background, spotlights fell on the large staircase that dropped majestically from the viewing gallery to the floor of the hall. The

288

sizeable waiting staff lined up in the gallery before charging down the stairs two by two, bodies perfectly upright, but legs blurring as they were glimpsed through the heavy banister. The effect was that of gliding, and not a speck of food was misplaced. As soon as the plates had been served, the waiters charged back up the stairs, narrowly missing the still-descending pairs of waiters. The precision was like that of a military aircraft display.

As the tables cleared, ours remained seated. Etienne called for champagne and we sat discussing the day and talking about the path that had brought us here. Etienne mentioned that he hadn't been at all sure about taking me on in the beginning, but that it was my persistence that eventually won through. He recalled asking Hervé what to do about this pestering Englishman who wanted some work experience and wouldn't leave him alone. Hervé had apparently advised him to 'take him on for some experience over Christmas. He'll have lost all enthusiasm for the career after that!'

Astoundingly, a disco ball made its appearance, music started playing and some of the remaining guests got up to dance. What music do they play at the Abbaye de Collonges?

You've guessed it: 'Gangnam Style'.

It was a long and extremely surreal night, but it was awesome, and the buzz of being introduced as the new Champion de France never diminished.

* * *

Fortunately, the next day was a Monday, so I had the chance for a lie-in — I needed it. I had slept poorly, unsure of what to make of this success and what it would mean for my future. As wonderful as this win was, it had never for a second been in the plan. The competition for me was primarily an opportunity for learning, and during the weeks of preparation I had never once considered what it would mean if I actually won the thing!

Life becomes more manageable with a strong coffee and a croissant, and that was exactly what I needed to get my mind back on track.

I immediately sent emails out thanking all who had helped me along the way and spoke to my friends and family to share the details and the good news. I confess that at that point I did also run a few vanity searches to see what the world was thinking. There was already a fair amount of noise on Facebook and I had received a big bump in my Twitter following.

Jen had done an internship with the *Independent* a few years previously, and it turned out that they were keen for an interview with me. Suddenly, the pressure was back on. This was it, the opportunity to start making a name for myself. I was certain that this piece in the *Independent* would be something small, just a little snippet about the fact I was the first foreigner ever to even *enter* the competition, let alone win. Even so, it would still be something that I could clip out and show a bank manager in the future when I wanted to start a cheese business of my own. I had to confess that I didn't quite feel ready for it, though. I had a fair bit of doubt as to whether my story was that interesting and warranted newspaper attention. Following Jen's guidance I answered the questions, trying not to be too modest so as to persuade the journalist to decide to look elsewhere for a story. Mainly, I talked about the cheeses themselves, why they were fascinating, and how much I loved the industry, rather than about myself.

Etienne meanwhile had sent me a text message: 'Matt, busy day tomorrow, let's start at five a.m.'

Normally we would be starting at six on a

Tuesday to receive the week's cheese delivery and get it all neatly checked and stored before attacking the restaurant orders. But, as the SIRHA was still going on in the background, there were a number of events that were keeping us extra busy. The cheese buffet for three hundred people that was due to take place the following evening was a prime example and would need considerable preparation as the cheese would all have to be pre-cut.

★ ★ ★

We were busy, but it was manageable. Jokes were made about my new status and everyone was generally jolly. Then, at around 9 a.m. the phone rang. It was the *Daily Mail*. Shortly followed by BBC World service, the *Telegraph* and *The One Show*.

I couldn't believe it. The *Independent* piece had been given pretty much the whole of the third page of the paper (the space was shared only with a small column about Iranian space monkeys) and my story had been picked up by Chris Evans's Radio 2 morning show. The phones continued to ring and everyone was asking for an interview. Panic started to set in as I realized that there was absolutely no way that I could keep on top of this. I was working flat out and both of the shop's phone lines were taken up by journalists. I called Jen, who had also been bombarded. She stepped in, taking some time off from her job, and becoming a query-fielding, interview-scheduling, social-media-managing, email-replying machine! I asked the rest of the team to forward all calls to her so that at least I could finish the work that needed doing, and made a mental note to buy her something very shiny to say thank you.

Much to her annoyance, Etienne started referring to her as my 'press secretary', before helpfully commenting that, when he had received similar attention on gaining his MOF status, his employer had given him time off to handle the attention.

'But unfortunately that won't be possible for you, as we're too busy.' Cheers, Etienne!

I ended up working through lunch trying to catch up on the time lost to conversations with journalists, and before long it was time to leave for the buffet. I had given around ten interviews and was a bit concerned that I couldn't remember whom they were all with. This Champion de France thing was going to take some getting used to.

The anxious waiting to see the finished articles would have to be put on hold, however, as we arrived and laid out our spread. The Mons big guns were out in force, Hervé himself was making an appearance. We had vast quantities of cheese and went all out on presentation, with milk churns, ferns, whole wheels of cheese and the smartest cheese jerkins that we could find. We definitely looked the part.

It was a fun evening. I spoke to a lot of people and was beginning to get a real sense of how interested people were in the fact that an Englishman had won a French cheese competition. As at the competition, there were a few raised eyebrows, but generally everyone was lovely.

★ ★ ★

At the beginning of that week, I have to admit, I held a significant animosity towards the press. It's a view that I've had for quite a while now and probably goes back to my scientific background and tendency towards objective measurability and rigorous cross-referencing of source material. I wasn't a fan of what I considered to be the nose-poking-trash-all-who-stand-in-your-way news-creating industry. I had believed that the UK papers would run fast and loose with my story, trying to blow it up into some kind of ridiculous statement about the relative merits of widely held stereotyped national identities — all with me lording it over the French in some kind of arrogant display of British fanaticism.

I will gladly admit that I was wrong to be worried. While there was some fishing for comments about the French being upset about my victory, most were happy to go with my personal view. I had stated that my win had little to do with being British. I'd come out to France as a keen consumer of quality cheese but with no relevant experience, let alone expertise. It was the training that I received in France, from experienced players in the French industry, that put me in a position to compete against, and on a good day to beat, those who had been raised in this land of cheese.

It would be unnecessarily modest not to personally claim some of the credit, but it was still clear that there is absolutely no way that I would have made it nearly so far without the support, encouragement and *savoir faire* of everyone I had encountered on this journey — in particular, Hervé, Etienne and François.

I felt that this spirit was reasonably well translated into print and, looking back in general over the articles, I see little that I regret. It was a crash course in media savvy, that's for sure, but I enjoyed the experience on the whole. There is one thing, though, that I regret.

I had entered the competition with the hope of being able to come out with my head held high and a nice picture of myself and the cheese platter. If anyone asked, I would just say that I had a place in the top sixteen of this national level competition and steer the conversation quickly to other topics (like Stilton).

I left the competition with first place, an unexpected but awesome result. However, in the excitement, I never got that nice photo. On scouring all of my memory cards and having asked all of my colleagues and friends, I discovered that the best photo of me and the platter that I could find was one which, while I would hate to sound vain in the slightest, does not exactly show my best side. Rather, it highlights my 'boggled-and-knackered-and-inexplicably-orange-tinted' side.

To anyone entering this kind of competition, I urge you to take heed and learn from my mistakes. Whether you're sweaty, exhausted or liberally splattered with cheese, you should always be ready for your close-up.

21

Onwards and Upwards

Life soon returned to a semblance of normality, although it was clear that the competition had left some lasting changes. I had a presence in the press, a full inbox, and a book contract. Almost overnight, I felt as though I had grown a little more industry clout.

I was under no illusion, though, that I still had an enormous amount more to learn and experience before I would feel truly comfortable using the title — if in fact I would ever learn to say the words 'Champion de France des Fromagers' without blushing at the sound of it. I needed to get back to work, and focus on the job in hand, learning as much as I could in the remaining time that I had in France. The plan was to stay at the shop until the end of May, at which point I would embark upon a succession of visits to some of the farms that supplied the Mons caves. An epically cheesy tour de France.

Jen had decided to return to London at the beginning of April, mainly to get back into her career, but also because she wasn't that keen on the idea of staying in France on her own while I was halfway up mountains, gallivanting with the sheep, cows and goats. I was sad about this of course, but I understood — her work life was just as important as mine, and sacrifices were required on both our parts.

We were determined to make the most of our remaining time together and planned a hectic schedule to try to take in the restaurants that we were still desperate to get to and the friends we wanted to see before we left.

*   *   *

Oh, did I mention my promotion?

During the Christmas period I had had independent meetings with both Etienne and Hervé at which I had enthused (potentially rather sickeningly) about how happy I was in the shop and about all the wonderful experience that I was getting. But in particular I mentioned how grateful I was that I hadn't been given sole responsibility of the *labo* and restaurant orders but had been able to rotate through all positions in the shop, working morning shifts one week and evening shifts the next and, most importantly, not being underground all day every day.

Less than a week later I found myself in a meeting with Hervé and Etienne at which they outlined their new vision for the coming year. I was to be responsible for the *labo* and the restaurant orders, I would be underground all day every day, with a brief respite at the weekends to make sure that I kept my hand in at sales. Sigh.

Of course I agreed. It was an important role: liaising with the caves in Saint-Haon (and our other suppliers) to buy in enough cheese for the shop, dealing with the restaurants that we supplied and being in charge of the cheese quality. This was one of those opportunities that would look really good on a CV. I mean, I'd be in charge of quality for a shop jointly owned by two MOFs. I knew, however, that it would be hard work with a fairly steep learning curve.

I wasn't wrong. The first cheese order that I placed took me about five hours, four of which were unpaid overtime. It was all rather fraught.

You have to buy enough cheese for the best part of a week. If you don't buy enough, you risk losing sales and potentially damage customer relations, particularly on the restaurant-order side. If you buy too much, you risk having to discount or, worse, bin.

The problem was that, being new to the task, I didn't really know how much cheese the shop sold from week to week, and the people who buy in bulk, the restaurants, mostly don't place their orders until after we've placed ours. So, exactly how many Brie did I need to order?

As it turned out, on that occasion I had overordered. It wasn't the end of the world — just a case of all hands to the pumps to shift that extra Brie!

Having had fair experience of the operations at the caves, I found it interesting to be on the receiving end. I quickly discovered that I didn't always get what I had ordered, and things that I hadn't ordered might occasionally find their way into the delivery. On top of this, there were significant differences in the ages of cheeses, which was only natural and a result of both the farmer delivering irregular quantities and the popularity of a given cheese with the other Mons shops and clients. It wasn't just a case of ensuring that we had the right quantity of cheese: it was also about the right *affinage*. Too young and it was unsaleable in the shop, too runny and it wouldn't be suitable for the restaurants.

These were things that were very difficult for me to control, and I learned that, upstairs in the shop, the team on the sales side could be very vocal when there were problems. We muddled through, though, and I was cut a bit of slack, although there was little remission from the teasing.

Once the all-consuming competition preparation had been consigned to history, I quickly started to feel much more on top of what I was doing. My relationships with the restaurants developed and we were getting better and better at satisfying their orders and suggesting interesting new cheeses. I was also getting better at what Etienne described as 'surgical ordering', ordering exactly the right quantities of cheese to satisfy demand. This helped us with our rotation, but also meant that we could be more reactive to the cheeses coming out of the caves, special offers that we could then share with our customers and interesting new products.

The initial stress of the job had dissipated and I came to understand that variations in ordering were manageable, and that the shop could adapt, like a well-oiled cheese machine, to peaks and troughs in quantities of specific cheeses and variances in their *affinage*. The benefit of having such a large range of cheeses was that if one was absent you could always propose something similar — except for the Boulette d'Avesnes, which was pretty rare. It's a bizarre cheese from the north of France made from the leftovers of Maroilles production, squashed by hand into a conical shape and flavoured with parsley, tarragon, cloves and paprika.

I will be honest and say that in the early days I would regularly sleep badly, tossing and turning, with thoughts of the shop's display being bare due to underordering or, worse, a cave full of rotting cheese, blue moulds spreading across the once-beautiful, cut, yellow faces of Comté, and Langres collapsing into a puddle as their orange rinds gave up against the pressure of their now fluid centre. I think it's fair to say that Jen was one of the main beneficiaries of my getting to grips with the job — simply in that she was less likely to be catapulted out of the bed by my wild, mid-cheese-nightmare thrashing about.

Of course, the job remained challenging, particularly with the fresh produce, such as milk, butter, cream, yoghurts and fresh cheeses. These had short shelf lives and highly unpredictable turnovers. Depending on the weather, a restaurant might order twenty Mozzarellas or none. It was a constant struggle but it meant there was a never a dull moment at work.

★ ★ ★

I didn't have much time to spend serving customers in the shop but I enjoyed it at the weekends and whenever I could spare the time during the week. Lots of our regular customers knew about the win and it was great to talk about it with them, particularly those who had supported me all through the training, and those who had been buying the crescent-shaped slices of Fourme de Montbrison and carved Mimolette for their cheese boards that I had made during practice runs of my platter.

I still had difficult clients, though, and I have to confess that there was no small amount of satisfaction when Victor would spot that I had a client who was concerned by my accent, and shout, 'Don't worry, madam, you're being served by the Champion de France!' It wasn't something that I was going to bring up myself, but I was more than happy for other people to do it.

★   ★   ★

In an attempt to both celebrate and capitalize on the win, Etienne wanted to run a cheese-and-wine evening that he had dubbed 'The Hundred Years War'. The idea was to have five pairings of cheeses, one English versus one French, and we would get the customers to vote for their favourites. This was fun to prepare, and I spent a long time picking over my choices (with a bit of help from the Neal's Yard team).

The evening was great and had garnered a decent level of interest, leaving us pretty much full. The British cheeses held up well, forcing a draw following the last-minute addition of a sixth round.

Some of the more interesting skirmishes of the night included an Innes log against a Sainte-Maure de Touraine. The former, light in texture with a flirtatious acidity, hailed from Staffordshire and was a surprise victor against its classic and much-loved French rival.

The Tunworth, a British take on the Camembert de Normandie, with a great flavour and delicate rind, notched up a close but still decisive win against its French counterpart, the original Camembert de Normandie, no less.

The Lancashire, unfortunately, and despite strong backing from me and the rest of the team, was less of a success, and our panel decided that, while they could see that it was a great cheese, the yoghurty taste to this British classic was just a bit too 'out there' for their palates. They voted the uncompromising and solidly French Salers to a near unanimous victory.

There were a young couple at the evening who had become regulars at these events. Michel was very tall and blonde, and his partner, Camille, was a dainty, petite brunette. They were good fun, and hung on every cheese-related word, the perfect audience. A few weeks later, following a rare sortie for myself (as I was at that point heavily involved in book writing and, in the absence of Jen, pretty much eschewing all human contact), I was heading back home on the Métro when I bumped into them. They let out great whoops and cheers and wouldn't stop telling everyone about my title as Champion de France until I had received an ovation from the whole train carriage.

I was flattered, but I could quite happily have curled up and died of embarrassment.

★ ★ ★

Seemingly before I could blink, it was mid-May and my last week in the shop. I had driven most of our possessions up to London for Jen, leaving the Lyon flat empty but for a few boxes to go into storage. I had performed my handover to Victor, who would be taking over my role in the shop. I saw in him the same uncertainty as I had had when I started it, but we had worked hard to make sure that I had shared everything that I had learned along the way. He would do a good job of it, and I could see that he had fresh ideas and an enthusiasm to develop himself and the business. My old domain would be in good hands.

I would miss the shop, a lot, and there had been many drawn-out goodbyes, but I knew instinctively that it wouldn't be the last time that I saw Etienne's team. Cheese was a small world, full of heart, and we were sure to bump into each other on a regular basis. We had shared some great moments together, some real triumphs, and they had all impacted heavily on my progress through the cheese world.

★ ★ ★

Shortly after the competition win, I had received an invitation from Lady Ricketts, the wife of the British Ambassador to France. They had heard of my success and were keen for me to visit them at the Residence in Paris, bearing a selection of the fine cheeses that had helped me make my mark in the competition. It goes without saying that I leaped at the chance, becoming ever more excited and nervous (in equal measure) as more and more details of the evening came to light — particularly the fact that this event would be attended by the Duchess of Cornwall and that, although there would be a number of other guests, many of whom were Brits who were making their mark in France, I would be the only one asked to provide any food.

The reception at the embassy was due to take place on the Monday following my last day at the shop and therefore would provide a neat segue between my life as a cheesemonger working for Etienne and my future, in all its opportunity-rich uncertainty. My preparations for the event were performed as for any other buffet that the shop might have catered for. I placed my order with the caves (and Neal's Yard), making it clear that this was a VIP event, and cared for the cheeses when they arrived as well as I could. Of course, I gave those pesky little Langres a lick of Marc de Bourgogne to perk them up a bit.

I was a little unsure as to how much cheese to bring, so I decided to make sure that there was enough for everyone to try at least one bit of each of the four cheeses that I would bring. This meant I'd need to create nearly five hundred individual cheese canapés on the morning of the event, as I wouldn't be able to pre-cut the day before or they would dry out.

I tried to come up with interesting flavour combinations and presentations, and eventually settled on bite-sized discs of a Bûchette de Manon — a small log-shaped goat's cheese from a brilliant producer in the south of France, not too far from Aix-en-Provence. To this creamy, zesty cheese I added a dollop of white-truffle-infused honey, and a sprinkling of winter savory. There were also my old friend the Langres, which we sliced thinly and served on rounds of baguette; a beautifully aged Comté, which I sliced painstakingly into matchsticks and laid out in a complex, geometric pattern on the wooden presentation board; and finally an Isle of Mull Cheddar. This raw-milk British representative had caught my attention. Using a method learned in Somerset it was made on a small island off the west coast of Scotland. It was a rather unusual cheese, pale in colour, and with a rich fruity taste with a slight, pleasant sting in the tail of its finish. Apparently, the lack of colour is partly due to the fact that the cows' diet includes draff, a by-product of the whisky industry that is low in the colour-giving carotenes found in grass.

Making the canapés in the prep kitchen of the embassy in Paris, while the butlers, florists and other staff whizzed around, was a surreal experience. Fortunately, I had my glamorous cheese assistant Jen to help me out or else I might never have got through the cutting of cheese, dolloping of honey or sprinkling of wild herbs.

For my first private commission, I felt that Jen and I had performed rather well. The cheeses looked great and, for the most part, they were polished off by the end of the evening. I hadn't embarrassed myself too badly and had met a lot of very lovely people, including a few celebrities, and a senior member of one of the government bodies that I had audited in my accounting days. (I decided to keep my auditor incarnation very quiet, and hoped that he wouldn't recognize me from my other life!) I thoroughly enjoyed the event in Paris, and it further confirmed that chatting about cheese and explaining to people how it's made and why it's special is something I want to do for the rest of my life.

★   ★   ★

All too soon, it was time to leave Lyon for good. Early one Sunday morning, I gave Audrey back the keys to the flat (she was in a mock sulk at us for daring to leave) and there was a cheque for our full deposit tucked neatly into my wallet. Life in Lyon was over.

It was time to leave the hustle and bustle of the country's gastronomic capital and to head into the mountains.

Summer had finally hit and the Lyonnais were taking full advantage, strolling stylishly along the banks of the rivers and chatting away in bars and cafés, whose tables spilled out onto the sun-warmed pavements. It was almost a year to the day that I had started working at the shop. I reflected that I had achieved more than I had ever imagined in my time there and I felt a warm sense of contentment that I could leave Lyon with my head held high.

But the career break was not yet over. It was time to meet the producers, the people who, far away from the glitz and glamour of Les Halles and the turmoil of the caves, were toiling away to make the cheese that I love. My schedule for farm visits was not yet complete: Hervé had put in a good word for me and I was hearing back all the time from some of the big names who were keen to work with me and show me what they do and why.

The lack of certainty didn't bother me; I was hitting the road, getting back to the countryside and seeing yet another side to the amazing richness and diversity that France had to offer.

My little car (lovingly named *Thunder-tank*) contained enough clothes to see me through a summer of hard graft, and enough enthusiasm to launch a new career.

Acknowledgements

Huge thanks to all those who made this book possible. There are many of you and you know what I'm like with names, so, if you aren't mentioned here, believe me, it wasn't personal!

I am massively grateful to both Hervé and Etienne for taking a chance on me and providing the training that allowed me to be useful in the industry. I am of course also grateful to the rest of the Mons family, in the caves and at the shop, for teaching me their trade. *Merci à vous tous!*

François needs to be thanked for his help in training for the competition and the NAO needs a mention for letting me come to France in the first place.

A huge debt is due to Louise Dixon and all of the wonderful people at Michael O'Mara Books for their help, support and advice.

And, of course, thank you to my family and friends for supporting me through the harder times and for never telling me that the whole thing was a big mistake.

Finally, Jen, thank you for being there with me the whole way. Your unending support has been amazing and I love you more than cheese.

★ ★ ★

For information about upcoming cheese events with Matt, or just to get in touch and say hello, check out www.thecheeseandi.blogspot.com.

We do hope that you have enjoyed reading this large print book.

Did you know that all of our titles are available for purchase?

We publish a wide range of high quality large print books including:
Romances, Mysteries, Classics
General Fiction
Non Fiction and Westerns

Special interest titles available in large print are:
The Little Oxford Dictionary
Music Book
Song Book
Hymn Book
Service Book

Also available from us courtesy of Oxford University Press:
Young Readers' Dictionary
(large print edition)
Young Readers' Thesaurus
(large print edition)

For further information or a free brochure, please contact us at:
Ulverscroft Large Print Books Ltd.,
The Green, Bradgate Road, Anstey,
Leicester, LE7 7FU, England.
Tel: (00 44) 0116 236 4325
Fax: (00 44) 0116 234 0205

HOPE IN A BALLET SHOE

Michaela & Elaine DePrince

In Sierra Leone, Mabinty Bangura — 'a girl with skin like the leopard' — is cherished and educated by her parents. Then the civil war rips her family apart: her father is murdered by rebels, and her mother sickens and dies. At just four years old, she is sent to an orphanage, where daily life can be harsh, and the violence outside presses ever closer. But one day, the Harmattan winds blow a magazine against the gates — its cover photograph showing a beautiful ballerina. Mabinty declares that, someday, she will dance like this lady, and be as happy . . .

REASONS TO STAY ALIVE

Matt Haig

'Far from the tunnel having light at the end of it, it seems like it is blocked at both ends, and you are inside it. So if I could only have known the future, that there would be one far brighter than anything I'd experienced, then one end of that tunnel would have been blown to pieces, and I could have faced the light . . . ' At the age of twenty-four, Matt Haig's world caved in. He could see no way to go on living. This is the true story of how he came through crisis, triumphed over the depression that almost destroyed him, and learned to live again.

THE CHEESE AND I

Accountant Matt Feroze had a dream
— to hang up his suit and immerse
himself in the highly competitive French
cheese industry. Taking a career break, he
packed his bags and set off to France
— saying goodbye to family, friends and a
reliable salary, and *bonjour* to milking
boisterous goats halfway up a mountain;
nurturing cheeses to their maturity; and
attempting to convince the local population that here indeed was an Englishman
capable of telling his Cheddar from his
Camembert. Then, for this self-described
'curd nerd', the months of hard work
invested in following his dream paid off
— Matt was soon being crowned *Champion de France des Fromagers* . . .